The Complete Guide to
Windsurfing

The Complete Guide to
Windsurfing

Jeremy Evans

Facts On File Publications
460 Park Avenue South
New York, N.Y. 10016

The Complete Guide to Windsurfing*
was conceived, edited and designed
by Holland & Clark Limited.

Photographer
Alastair Black.
Designer
Julian Holland
Editor
Philip Clark
Artist
Nicholas Hall

Published in the United Kingdom in 1983 by
Evans Brothers Limited, Montague House,
Russell Square, London WC1B 5BX,
England.

Published in the United States of America in
1983 by Facts On File, Inc.,
460 Park Avenue South, New York, N.Y. 10016.

Library of Congress Cataloging in Publication
Data
Evans, Jeremy
  Windsurfing: the complete guide to
  windsurfing

  Includes index.
  1. Windsurfing. I. Title
GV811.63E83 1983   797.1.'72   82-21117
ISBN 0-87196-248-9

*Windsurfer® and Windsurfing® are
registered trademarks of Windsurfing
International of Marina Del Rey, Calif.

Typesetting by Tradespools Limited
Frome, Somerset
Reproduction by Dot Gradations Limited,
Southend.
Printed and bound in Spain by
Printer industria gráfica sa
Sant Vicenç dels Horts, Barcelona, 1983
Depósito legal B. 1865-1983

Contents

Part One

Part Two

Windsurfing for Beginners

How did windsurfing begin, and how has it developed during its first 20 years?

What are the different types of boards, and how do you tell which one to buy?

What is the basic theory behind windsurfing, and how do you learn to master the initial stages?

When the wind starts blowing a little harder, how do you handle it; and when you get into trouble how do you look after yourself?

These and many other questions are answered in the following pages.

Basic Windsurfing Glossary

THE BOARD

Nose
Front end, or bow.

Stern
Back end.

Skeg
Small fin at the stern, to keep the board sailing straight.

Daggerboard
Large fin mid-way, which is removable from the daggerboard case. Prevents the board going sideways. A storm daggerboard is shorter, and makes the board easier to control in strong winds.

Shims
Friction pads to ensure the daggerboard fits tightly in its case.

Mast foot well
Circular or T-shaped well just forward of the daggerboard case.

Towing eye
In the nose of the board. To take a towing line.

THE RIG (moving upwards)

Mast foot
Fits into the mast foot well, and is normally permanently attached to the universal joint which allows the rig to be swung through 360 degrees and inclined through a minimum of 180 degrees. The mast foot/universal joint is the adaptor between the rig and the board.

Downhaul line
Attaches the *tack* (bottom left hand corner) of the sail to the mast foot.

Wishbone
The boom, made from two elliptical alloy tubes with plastic end fittings.

Inhaul line
Attaches the wishbone to the mast.

Outhaul line
To pull the *clew* (far right hand corner) of the sail out to the end of the wishbone.

Uphaul rope
To pull the rig up out of the water. Attached to the mast foot by the shockcord.

Battens
Flat pieces of flexible fibreglass used to support the *roach* of the sail – the area outside an imaginary straight line drawn between the clew and the top of the sail (*head*). The camber is the amount of curve in the sail – ie the area between an imaginary straight line drawn from the clew to the mast, and the sail. The camber determines whether the sail is trimmed full or flat.

TYPES OF BOARD

Flatboard
A board with an underwater profile that is more or less flat, and therefore stable. Ideal as an all-round board – for general multi-purpose use.

Roundboard
A racing board with an underwater profile that is round, and therefore unstable. Also called a displacement board.

Funboard
A board specifically intended for strong winds. Also called a strong wind board.

SAILING TERMS
GENERAL

Starboard
Right (looking forward).

Port
Left (looking forward).

Windward
The side the wind is blowing from.

Leeward
The side the wind is blowing to.

POINTS OF SAILING

Leeway
Making leeway – the amount the board moves sideways, or to leeward.

Close hauled
Sailing as close to the wind as possible.

Reaching
Sailing with the wind on the beam – ie with the wind at or near 90 degrees to the board's course.

Running
Sailing with the wind directly, or almost directly behind.

ALTERING COURSE

Bearing off
Sailing away from the wind (by inclining the rig forward).

Heading up
Sailing up towards the wind (by inclining the rig aft, ie towards the stern).

Tacking
Altering course so the nose of the board passes through the eye of the wind – ie the direction the wind is coming from.

Gybing
Altering course so the stern passes through the eye of the wind.

Luffing
Letting out the sail, or heading up so that the wind strikes the leeward side of the sail and causes it to lift or *back* (flutter).

WEATHER AND SEA CONDITIONS

Beaufort Scale
Measurement of wind speed based on knots – nautical miles per hour. A nautical mile equals about 1.85 km.

Apparent Wind
The wind that is experienced by the sailor – different in direction and speed from the True Wind experienced by a stationary observer.

Onshore Wind
Wind blowing away from the shore.

Tide
Coastal movement of the sea induced by pull of the sun and moon. Tide rip is when it runs extremely fast round a headland or in a confined area.

RACING

One-Design
A class of identical boards – eg the Windsurfer Regatta.

Open Class
Different boards racing together to the same design and construction rules. Open Class Division 1 is for flatboards; Open Class Division 2 is for roundboards.

Olympic Triangle
The normal racing course as used by dinghies.

Long Distance
A long race which normally features a Le Mans start and concentrates on reaching legs.

Slalom
Two boards racing one another around a short course of buoys.

Freestyle
A tricks routine.

Ins-and-outs
Racing in-and-out through the surf, best suited to strong winds.

Pentathlon
A mix of all or some of: triangle; long distance; slalom; freestyle; and ins-and-outs.

Weight Groups
Division of competitors by weight for triangle racing.

IYRU
International Yacht Racing Union.

IBSA
International Boardsailing Association.

The elements of a windsurfer are common to most marques and models, particularly if they are of the flatboard/allround type illustrated here. You may find slight general differences in specification and design, and more marked differences with parts such as the daggerboard, skeg, and mast foot, but once you can recognize the parts on one board you will be able to recognize them on any board.

Mast tip

Head

Leech

Class insignia

Sleeve

Batten pocket with batten

Luff

1947

Rubber bumper with inhaul

Boom end fitting

Inhaul with cleat

Clew

Window

Uphaul

Outhaul with cleat

Foot

Tack

Wishbone (boom)

Downhaul

Mast

Shockcord

Daggerboard case

Stern

Nose

Skeg

Alternative mast foot well

Mast foot with universal joint

Daggerboard

The Background

In just over a decade windsurfing has become one of the most successful new sports of the century. From a couple of people experimenting with surfboards in California, it has turned into a multi-million dollar industry enjoyed by Americans, Europeans, Asians and Australians. Its success has been recognized by its inclusion in the 1984 Olympic Games in Los Angeles.

Windsurfing can be enjoyed in any place where there is sufficient water – be it open sea or a tiny lake – and in most weather conditions. True it's most fun when you do it somewhere warm with a fair wind, but so long as the ice is thin enough to break, enthusiasts will even windsurf right through a Scandinavian winter. A fair wind means the wind that suits you best, and this may mean anything from a light breeze to a howling Force 6.

Given the right equipment, there are few days when a windsurfer can't go out – no wind at all is a far more likely reason than too much of it.

There is no doubt that from the point of view of physical fitness, it is young people who take to windsurfing with the greatest ease. The peak age for top racers is late teens to a maximum of 25, after which they go downhill rapidly! However, the same is true of tennis and snow ski-ing, and with the right equipment a grandfather or an eight-year-old can still have plenty of fun.

Nor should cost be a problem. You can buy a good new board for a few hundred dollars or pounds in most countries, and if you can't afford that, there are plenty around secondhand.

Of course, you can spend a lot more on your board or boards (a real enthusiast will probably own three or four) and the same goes for the incidental costs. Unless you're lucky enough to live in the tropics, you will need a neoprene wetsuit to keep warm, and you may wish to add boots, harness, and a dry suit to the list.

Lastly, you'll need to transport the board, and unless you live right by the water's edge, that means a car with a roof rack. However, it's not always necessary to buy one. You can always share the roof space of a fellow enthusiast.

Learning
All beginners feel incredibly stupid when first having a go at windsurfing. Falling off every five seconds, they swear it's the most difficult thing they've ever done, and if that's when they give up, they carry on believing it.

However, it's not. With proper tuition (see pages 32–35) there are very few people who are incapable of windsurfing – about as many as are incapable of riding a bicycle. A two week holiday in the sun is enough time for anyone to get reasonably proficient, and in that time, those who have a good sense of balance and are reasonably fit, should be well on the way to handling stronger winds.

Advanced Techniques
Windsurfing doesn't stop when you can sail without falling off the boards.

A variety of conditions and types of boards give the sport almost unlimited possibilities. Apart from boards for general use, there are boards for racing, and boards for strong winds and waves with a variety of rigs (more cost!) These are constantly being developed and uprated, and demand board handling techniques that must improve by the day.

Most people are happy enough to restrict windsurfing to their family holidays and occasional weekends, but for those who aspire to world class regatta sailing, or jumping the waves off Hawaii, the sport must become the main reason for their existence.

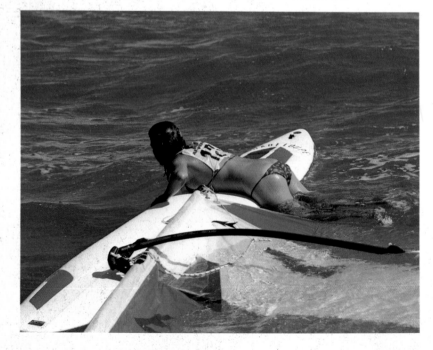

Left: This is how we all start! Undignified, but easier if the water is warm (Guadeloupe here), and lots of fun to come.

Right: Windsurfing into the sunset with a nice breeze at the end of a hot day. Nothing could be better therapy after work in the office – if you're near the water.

Hoyle Schweitzer

The first published account of windsurfing occurred in August 1965. The American magazine *Popular Science* ran a feature on a 'sailboard' designed by a Mr Newman Darby ...'A Sport So New That Fewer Than 10 People Have Yet Mastered It'. You would hardly recognize it as a board today. The shape was primitive, and the square-rigger type of sail set it well apart from the board that actually caught on.

This prototype was developed by two Californians – Hoyle Schweitzer and Jim Drake. The latter was an aeronautical engineer who hit on the idea of an articulated rig. This led in turn to the universal-joint mast foot system that is used on the Windsurfer and its derivatives today – Windsurfer with a capital *W* is the brand name of board that resulted from the work of these two men: *windsurfing* or *boardsailing* is the generic name for sailing it.

On 26 April 1969 Drake presented a paper at a technical symposium on sailboat design, entitled *Windsurfing – A New Concept In Sailing*. It revealed that he and

Left: A jovial Jim Drake on the beach in Hawaii, looking at developments in the Pan Am Cup. Although with no commercial interest in windsurfing, he still shows up at regattas.

In the early days of board development, he experimented with a mast rigidly attached to the daggerboard which could only move fore and aft – his articulated universal joint represented the vital breakthrough.

Above: Hoyle Schweitzer sitting on a pile of cases containing his Windsurfers (for the 1980 World Championship in the Bahamas). He developed the hot moulded polyethylene method of construction for the board, which is used by his Licensees in the Netherlands (the biggest), Japan, and Australia. All Hoyle's family windsurf – his eldest son Matt has long been rated one of the best in the world.

Schweitzer had tried out a number of designs. A year later Schweitzer had them in limited production.

The Windsurfer

The Windsurfer was the first board to go into production, but with Schweitzer's limited financial resources it was the Europeans who paved the way for the sport's present-day popularity.

The large Dutch textile manufacturer Ten Cate heard of the Windsurfer in 1970, and sent representatives to see Schweitzer with the idea of selling him sailcloth. That deal was never completed, but they came back with 100 of his boards. The following year the quantity was upped to 1000, and 3000 the one after. The US production couldn't keep up with this demand, so armed with a licence to manufacture, Ten Cate set up their own factory in Holland. They still have the biggest market share.

Right: Newman Darby's board had a very different rig. The early windsurfer prototypes looked fairly primitive, but one cannot imagine this rig ever being as efficient upwind. It has been resurrected in recent years to prove 'prior art' in the legal proceedings concerning Schweitzer's Patent in Germany, and the UK with Peter Chilvers'. It never had any great commercial success, and Newman Darby lives quietly in the USA.

The Patent

In 1968 Hoyle Schweitzer and Jim Drake filed an application for a Patent to cover their invention in the USA.

Shortly afterwards Hoyle bought out full interest in the project to go it alone, and also filed his Patent in the countries where he thought his Windsurfer would be most successful – the UK, West Germany, Australia, Japan and Canada – he had to be selective as he couldn't afford to apply to every country in the world.

Since that time, the success of windsurfing, which has led to it being copied worldwide, has also led to considerable legal wranglings for Hoyle Schweitzer. He has never been able to exercise any control over what goes on in the 'unpatented territories', notably France, but where his Patent holds sway he has granted licences to produce boards built and designed by other manufacturers.

In return for their licences, these companies agreed to pay Schweitzer a royalty of approximately 7.5 per cent on every board. Not surprisingly, several other major manufacturers were unwilling to pay this amount, or in some cases were unable to get a licence agreement.

Their boards flooded the German market putting the licensed boards at a disadvantage, but after long-drawn-out court cases German Law upheld the Patent in 1980.

The same problems were deliberated over in British courts in

The original Patent document that started it all. Patent litigation has tended to rest on the wishbone and universal joint. On the whole, the Patent issue has been successfully overcome, with compromise on both sides.

PATENT SPECIFICATION

(11) 1 258 317

DRAWINGS ATTACHED

(21) Application No. 10919/69 (22) Filed 28 Feb. 1969
(31) Convention Application No.
716 547 (32) Filed 27 March 1968 in
(33) United States of America (US)
(45) Complete Specification published 30 Dec. 1971
(51) International Classification B 63 h 9/08
(52) Index at acceptance
B7V 72 73
B7B 244 423

(54) WIND-PROPELLED VEHICLE

(71) We, HENRY HOYLE SCHWEITZER AND JAMES ROBERT DRAKE of 317 Beirut, Pacific Palisades, California, United States of America and 385 Mesa Road, Santa 5 Monica, California, United States of America respectively; both citizens of the United States of America do hereby declare the invention, for which we pray that a patent may be granted to us, and the 10 method by which it is to be performed, to be particularly described in and by the following statement: —

The field of art to which the invention pertains includes the field of ships, par-15 ticularly sailboats and iceboats, and the field of land vehicles with sail propulsion.

Sail propulsion has been suggested as a motive means not only for boats and iceboats, but also for such watercraft as surf-20 boards and landcraft such as sleds, i.e. generally any lightweight small craft. Typically, a sail is provided on a mast that is rigidly secured to the craft in a vertical position and additionally the sail and mast 25 can be entwined in a network of riggings and control mechanisms.

The general effect of providing a sail on a normally sailfree vehicle is to convert the vehicle into a water or land-boat. Thus, 30 by rigidly securing a sail to a surfboard, the feel of the surfboard and enjoyment as such is lost and the skill normally required to control it is no longer needed. Instead one obtains the speed and feels of a light 35 sailboat and needs substantially only those skills appropriate to control a sailboat. The same "denatur..." occurs with other vehicles modifi... ...ear a sail.

A problem a... ...n a sail is fitted to 40 a vehicle that ... have high roll stability in that ... ...cessive winds can overturn th...

A need there... ...afely providing wind-pro... ...a vehicle 45 not normally so... ...means

preserves the original ride and control characteristics of the vehicle.

In accordance with the present invention there is provided a wind-propelled vehicle comprising body means, an unstayed spar 50 connected to said body means through a joint which will provide universal-type movement of the spar in the absence of support thereof by a user of the vehicle, a sail attached along one edge thereof to the 55 spar, and a pair of arcuate booms, first ends of the booms being connected together and laterally connected on said spar, second ends of the booms being connected together and having means thereon connected to the 60 sail such that said sail is held taut between the booms.

In particular embodiments, the spar is connected to the vehicle body by means of a universal joint, i.e. a joint having three 65 axes of rotation.

The pair of arcuate booms are provided laterally disposed on the spar to hold the sail taut and provide a hand hold for the 70 user.

The invention can be used on watercraft, iceboats and landcraft. It can be used on small yachts, runabouts, canoes, rowboats, and other such craft, but is most 75 advantageously used on small and lightweight vehicles such as surfboards, iceboats, and sleds. Leeboards can be provided for a watercraft of low roll stability such as a surfboard. The term "leeboard" 80 used in the specification and claims is meant to include center boards and dagger-boards, as these terms are known to the sailing art, as well as other projections from the body of the craft, planar or otherwise extending 85 into or onto the water for stabilization.

The present invention allows essentially all of the steering and control to be accomplished through the sail; i.e. no rudder or other steering mechanism is needed, although such need not be excluded. One may 90

1982, and the net result in both countries was a certain amount of compromise on both sides. Many manufacturers agreed to honour his royalty terms, and Schweitzer took a far easier line on granting licences to those who required them.

Apart from a dedicated minority of windsurfing 'superstars', the USA remained largely uninterested in windsurfing until the early 1980s. Then, having swamped their own countries, the European manufacturers began an onslaught across the Atlantic, with extensive Patent litigation resulting once again – which was doubly acrimonious with the first windsurfing Olympics being held in Los Angeles.

European Manufacturers

Once the Windsurfer began to catch on in Europe, rival manufacturers were not slow to join in the new craze.

Windglider was started by German entrepreneur Fred Ostermann in 1975, followed by the Swiss Mistral company in 1976. Hi Fly, Sailboard (both German), and Dufour (French) followed, and these are now the major manufacturers. Between them they swamped the two biggest markets – Germany and France – with a total of over 250,000 boards by 1982, before transferring their interests to the USA which suddenly opened up as the virgin land of windsurfing. The UK remains a poor relation with maximum board sales of around 30,000.

Besides these big mass-volume manufacturers, there are hundreds and probably thousands of other companies producing boards – some with the capacity for several thousand units per year, others just turning out custom made boards at the rate of two or three per month. In France alone there may be 200 or more manufacturers, and Far Eastern countries are busy turning out replicas of European boards.

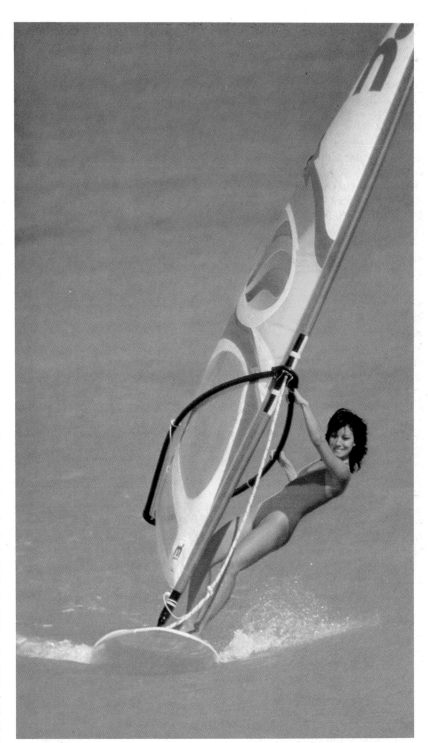

As one of the world's largest windsurfer manufacturers, the Swiss Mistral company remained unlicensed until 1981, when due to the Patent action in the German courts they had to pay large amounts of back royalties. Schweitzer subsequently eased up considerably on his policy of granting licenses.

Windsurfing Today

From Schweitzer's first boards, windsurfing has evolved rapidly in a variety of directions – in some cases it has turned back full circle to being a surfboard with a sail!

However, for most people a sailboard is something for occasional use. They haven't the time or the inclination to get involved with the more rarified aspects of sport, and the great mass of the market is, and always will be, served by the general purpose all-round 'flatboard' that every major manufacturer has within its range.

The Windsurfer, the Mistral Competition, the Dufour Wing, the Sea Panther – these and hundreds of other brands are flat, stable boards of similar length. Their price and performance are closely allied, and in many cases it is only the striping on their hulls, or the company's aggressive marketing policy, that sets them apart.

The Next Stage
Once bitten, some want to progress a little further than enjoyment on the occasional weekend. They can either turn to racing, or to a style of sailing which is orientated to mastering stronger winds.

Racing
A windsurfer performs as well as any dinghy, and racing and regattas are now a popular part of the windsurfing scene.

You can go racing in the evenings after work, travel across the country for a weekend national event, or across the world for a week-long international championship.

The most popular marques have their own one-design events, while most other flatboards are suitable for beginners' racing. The more experienced sailors will turn to 'roundboards', the Grand Prix section of windsurfing, called IYRU Division 2.

These roundboards race in similar events to the flatboards, but are

Above: Taking off – on a Mistral Takeoff – near Diamond Head, Hawàii. Few windsurfers have the ability to sail like this.

part of an *Open Class* designed specifically for triangle racing – the Sailboard Race, Turbo, Jet GTI, and Mistral M1 are popular examples. They are very fast, but considerably more difficult to sail, owing to their unstable shape.

Stronger Winds
As their techniques improve, sailors find that they can master stronger winds. At the same time the necessary windsurfing equipment is being improved all the time.

For most people, the best boards for strong winds are flatboards. They are easy to control, and with the addition of design details such as footstraps, and special daggerboards, skegs, and rigs, are marketed solely for sailing in winds of Force 4+.

All the developments in this part of the market have been led by the highly romanticized sailors of Hawaii, immortalized in thousands of colour photos, leaping skywards from the waves.

The Record Breakers
The types of boards available have multiplied rapidly, and so have the variety of disciplines within the sport.

There are now special strong wind regattas where you can't race if the wind is less than Force 4; wave jumping competitions where the sailors are judged on style and achievements; and speed trials where boards sail timed runs through a 500 metre course in the hope of breaking a world record.

In the past three years, boards have sailed round Cape Horn (Frederic Beauchêne); across the Pacific and the Baring Straits between America and Russia (Baron Arnaud de Rosnay); around Great Britain (the Sea Panther team); and across the Atlantic (Christian Marty and Frederic Giraldi). It is a tribute to their organization and common sense that the number of fatalities and casualties generally has remained small.

Escalating Costs
As the disciplines within the sport have grown, so has the cost. It's no problem if you stick with your learner's flatboard, but one day you may find you need: a one-design flatboard for racing; a roundboard for Open Class racing; and a board with footstraps for strong wind sailing. You will also need a variety of sails and accessories to go with them, and in a highly commercial business you will find that when you are racing you are up against professionals.

Windsurfing has become far more professional than sailing. All the major manufacturers pay top sailors to help market their products, and there are now an increasing number of events with cash prizes – the sailors get out what they put in.

Right: All most of us want is a nice breeze, hot sun, and a board that's not too demanding to sail.

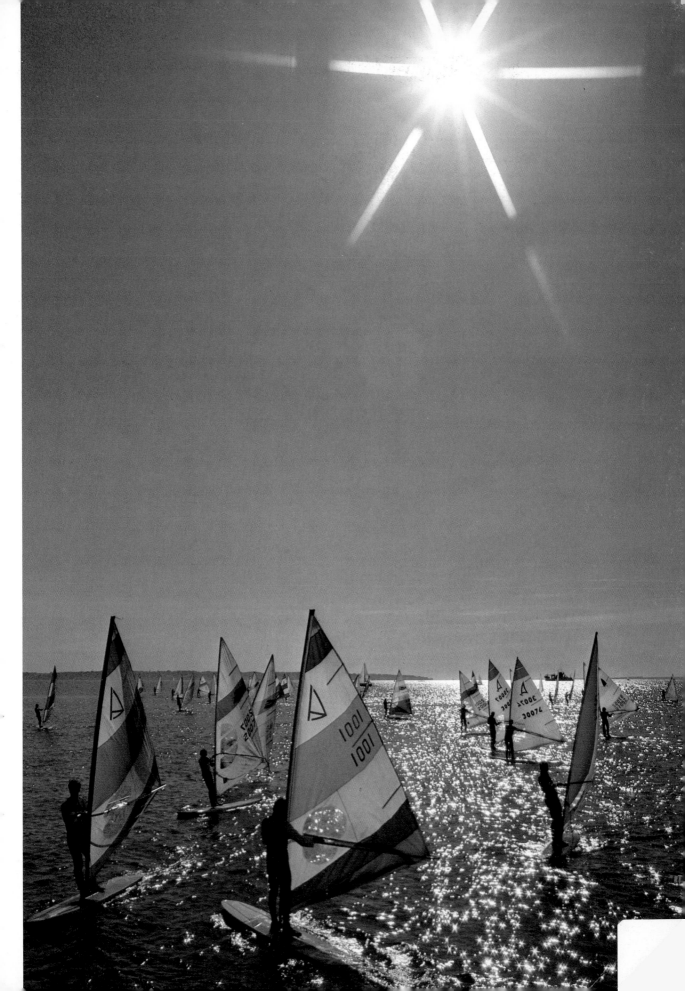

Types of Boards

The five boards on these pages cover most aspects of the sport.

A professional might well have one of each, and a great many more besides. He would also be changing and updating them at least once a season. More than likely he would be supported by a manufacturer, otherwise he would have to spend a great deal of money.

Most of these boards are turned out on production lines by the major manufacturers, though the very specialized ones are often hand built. For instance, a wave jumping board currently being shaped in Hawaii won't be in full stream production with a major manufacturer for at least another six months, and then will rapidly be outdated by another new shape.

However, whether or not a board is of the most up-to-the-minute design is largely irrelevant to all but the most enthusiastic and advanced sailors. The major manufacturers offer a well-presented product which is simply a variation of that offered by their competitors. Every now and again one manufacturer gains a temporary advantage, but construction and marketing techniques are so sophisticated that there really is little to choose between the different products.

One should also remember that the five categories of boards represented here overlap. The sailor who is addicted to the short pintail speedboard (E) is unlikely to own the far easier to sail funboard (D) (though the reverse is quite likely to be the case when the sailor is not confident enough to manage his most difficult board in all conditions). Some manufacturers also have flatboards that convert into strong wind boards – and some of these have many of the hull characteristics of roundboards.

Allround Flatboard
The type of board that started it all, the best to start on, and the most popular for allround use. Flat, stable, and forgiving, almost every manufacturer has a board like this in his range.

Normal dimensions are: around 380 cm long; weighing about 19 kg; with a sail between 5 and 6.5 sq m. Material could be polyethylene, ABS, or fibreglass. Typical examples are the Windsurfer, Mistral Competition, Windglider, Sea Panther – and many more.

Pan Am Strong Wind Board
Through the Pan Am Cup in Hawaii, a type of board has evolved which can be raced in winds over Force 4. Similar in shape to the board above, it will have more rocker; a bigger skeg area; a daggerboard case that is further aft with a shorter daggerboard; and footstraps. Easy to sail and safe for strong wind enjoyment – typical examples are the Windsurfer Rocket, Mistral Naish, TC Hunter, and Laser Funbird.

IYRU Division 2 Roundboard

The Open Class roundboard is the Grand Prix racing board, with the most advanced design characteristics. These boards are for triangle racing only – they are tricky to sail owing to their rounded shape, and tricky to manufacture down to the weight limit of 18 kg.

At major championships, most of the manufacturers display specially built examples, most of which are too fragile to sell to the public.

Strong Wind/Funboard

For wave jumping and strong wind fun, a short board (290–330 cm compared to the 380 cm Pan Am board opposite) that has three or four skegs for lateral resistance, or a retracting daggerboard. Buoyant, stable, and easy to control – but only suitable for winds of Force 4+ – great care needs to be taken in getting back upwind after a long and exciting broad reach. Rigs will be interchangeable with other boards. Sailboard Fun is a typical example.

Sinker

The extreme surfboard for real experts evolved in Hawaii in 1981. Very short (say 260 cm), light (10 kg maximum) and with minimal buoyancy (water starts and high speed power gybes) boards like this are invariably built one-off by very small concerns or individuals. Simply a shaped foam block covered in glassfibre or something like Kevlar, it will have one to three skegs and footstraps, with the mast foot located forward.

One-Designs

The most numerous racing classes worldwide are the flatboard one-designs, lead by the Windsurfer, Windglider, and Mistral, which have all been dubbed International Classes by the International Yacht Racing Union (IYRU).

There are several other one-design classes that race in various countries – assembling a one-design fleet is quite simply a matter of getting enough identical boards that can be raced together. In the UK the British-built Sea Panther has a strong one-design following, while on the Continent the Sailboard Company organizes one-design roundboard regattas. Similarly one can find one-design racing for Dufour and Hi Fly boards, but most windsurfing countries still have the three major classes.

A one-design class will have its own class association. If it's a big enough class it will also have enough money – either from the manufacturer or from a commercial sponsor – to be able to provide a wide variety of services for its members.

Above: The Windsurfer is the biggest of the one-designs, as well as the most widespread. Built in supertough polyethylene, it is as popular as ever, and a notably good board in stronger winds and waves. World Championships have been held in Sardinia, Mexico, the Bahamas, and Japan – anywhere that is exotic.

Left: The Mistral Competition Light is the third biggest OD in the world. Of the three International Classes it is probably the most refined – and the most expensive. Built in epoxy it weighs 18 kg, while an almost identical version (the Club) is built in polyethylene and weighs 23 kg. A 'Superlight' weighs 15 kg.

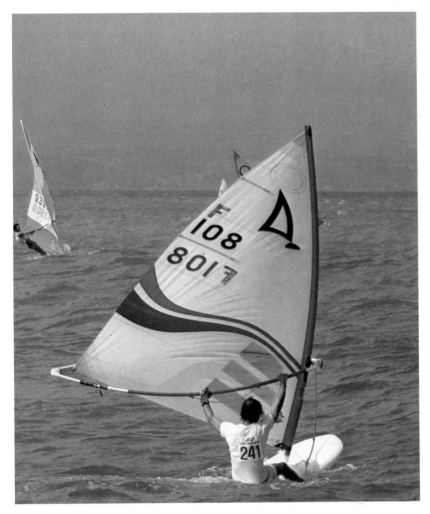

The Olympic Windglider sailing downwind in difficult conditions – or perhaps the driver just wanted a rest. Controversy has surrounded the choice of this board as the first to take part in an Olympic regatta.

For a small membership fee a member can expect: 1. A regular monthly newsletter containing information on events. 2. A chance to advertize secondhand equipment. 3. The offer of an advantageous insurance deal. 4. Regular regattas, on a local or national basis. 5. Class association get-togethers – perhaps a film show in the winter. 6. The chance to qualify for international regattas, with costs paid by a sponsor.

In addition, the most popular one-designs are able to offer: local racing on summer evenings and weekends; weekend national events; and week long European and World Championships.

All the racing tends to be based on the Olympic triangle where possible, though with reasonably short legs so that races in a fair wind last well under an hour. A typical weekend or week long event will have five or six identical races with an Olympic scoring system deciding the eventual winners.

Only with a very small entry will there be a single winner, as most of the one-design classes are divided into 'weight groups'. Given the same ability, a lighter sailor will travel faster than a heavier one, particularly when the board lacks buoyancy and is pushed down into the water by weight. So, to prevent the lightweights winning every race, Windsurfers class racing, for instance, is divided into a total of five groups with five overall separate placings. The sailors are weighed before the event and are divided into: light; light-medium; medium-heavy; and heavy – plus a separate group for ladies. (Other classes may only have two weight groups).

There is seldom an overall winner of the triangle racing, but these events also tend to feature several other types of competition, and sometimes have an overall 'pentathlon' winner.

The 'freestyle' is a three-minute routine for the sailor to show off his tricks on the board. A very rarefied skill, it has become so competitive that some sailors specialize in this alone.

'Slalom' is a knock-out competition for two boards on a short slalom course, depending on skill in quick tacking and gybing.

The 'Long Distance Race' is, as its name implies, a race of considerable length (anything up to 25 miles), frequently with a Le Mans style 'beach start' and long reaching legs.

The Olympics

In 1980 the IYRU chose the Windglider as the first board to race in the 1984 Olympics in Los Angeles.

Unfortunately the choice had political overtones. Even though the Windsurfer had more widespread support and popularity worldwide, the Windglider was the only likely contender being built behind the Iron Curtain (in Hungary).

Hoyle Schweitzer was of course extremely unhappy, particularly when the Olympics were due to be held on his back door with someone else's board.

Open Class

The IYRU Open Class Division 2 rules are set out in detail in the Glossary at the end of the book. In brief they require a board of maximum length (390 cm); minimum weight (18 kg); and maximum depth (22 cm) – though this ruling was only introduced after the European Championship in 1980.

They also require a sail shape which is virtually standard (approximately 6.3 sq m maximum), and prohibit the use of 'exotic' materials.

The Boards
These rules are surprisingly tight and have led to look-alike roundboards since the Tornado first appeared, and won the European Championship in 1979.

Designers discovered that the key to speed was a very buoyant board with the least possible wetted area, which would plane long before a flatboard on any point of sailing. Once they caught on to this principle, they made even thicker boards, so that some boards at the European Championship of 1980 were deeper than they were wide –

with the result that they were very difficult to sail, and hopeless in strong winds.

The 22 cm maximum depth measurement resulted, and now it is difficult to tell the hull shape of one roundboard from another. There may be a little more buoyancy or rocker here or there, but whether the winner is a Sailboard Race, a Turbo, a Lechner, or a TC Win (all designed or copied from the same designer, George Lechner) they all look much the same.

Events
The boards even perform similarly but the difference comes at an important regatta when the manufacturers show up with 'specials'.

Since its inception, most of the major manufacturers have used the Open Class as their showcase. A win is the most effective piece of marketing in a sport-cum-industry where 'image' is so important, and manufacturers patronize major events with full works teams.

Of course, none of the sailors would actually admit to being professional (which would be prohibited under IYRU rules), but in the top teams it is common knowledge that competitors race with a cash incentive and have a hefty retainer

from the manufacturer, while those not quite in the top league expect free equipment and all expenses paid.

Nor would the manufacturers admit to the boards being different from the ones they sell in the shops. In many cases they are not, but with the requirements of mass production there are problems with roundboard manufacture which can only be overcome by specialization. For example, the more volume a roundboard has, the faster it will go. Within the 22 cm limit, the maximum volume is about 325 litres, but then keeping the board down to the 18 kg weight maximum requires a skilfully applied and very thin glassfibre skin, which cannot be exactly duplicated by mass production techniques.

Division 1
In 1980 the IYRU introduced the idea of a new Division 1 for flatboards. They reasoned that since these were the boards that the great majority of sailors owned, there should be a class to cater for them.

The rules are in essence the same as Division 2, except that there is a maximum depth measurement of 16.5 cm – the three International Classes are automatically included.

Left: Open Class racing with Karl Messmer (Mistral M1) to windward of two Windglider Mach 1's and a French Crit. Messmer won the Open Class World title in 1981 before transferring his interests to jumping waves in Hawaii.

Right: The early pacemaker in Open Class design was the Alpha Professional, with its chine shaped hull. Its last successful appearance at a major event was the Open Class European Championship of 1979, when it finished second and fourth, bracketed by the first of the roundboards that displaced it – the Austrian Tornado.

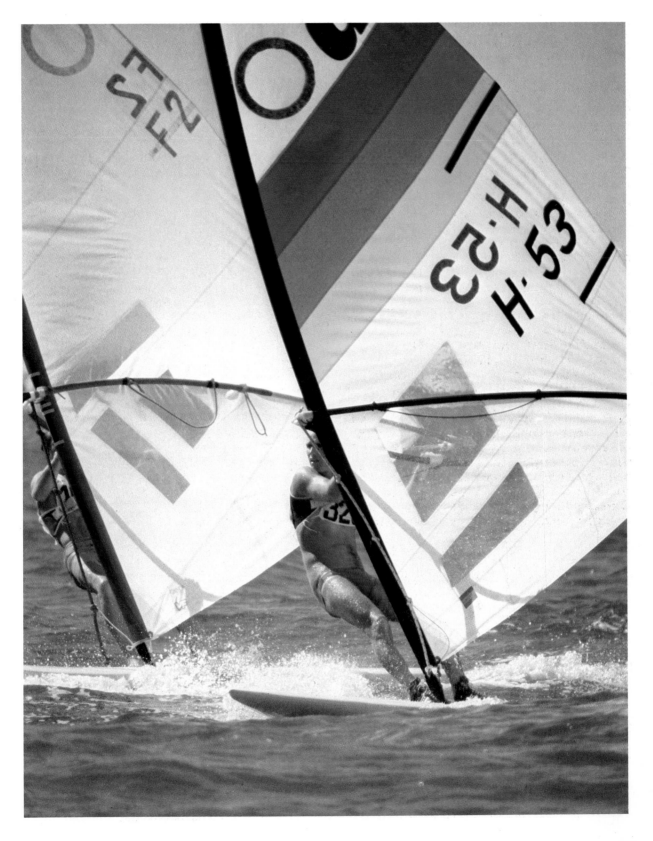

The Professionals

Despite overlooking the fact that a great many 'amateurs' are very obviously professionals, the IYRU and various national authorities (such as the RYA in the UK) take a firmer stand over the question of advertizing.

Advertizing contravenes their Rule 26, for racers are not allowed to wear a sponsor's logo on their clothing or sails, and the boards themselves can only have their brand names in the very smallest lettering.

However, the sport has reached the stage where many of these undeclared professionals have got used to making a very good living from it, and, with their sponsors, would be happy to see the creation of a purely professional circuit, along the lines of the world's top tennis and golf tournaments.

This idea has been slow to materialize, perhaps partly because it's not the easiest sport to televize, and is not readily comprehensible to a layman.

However, in the UK, self-declared 'subsidized' boardsailors have received cash prizes for winning races at a national level since 1981, and that year also featured the start of an annual circuit of major professional regattas.

These events – organized by a former major influence on the IBSA, Will Sutherland – require the competitors to flaunt their own sponsors, and the company backing the event, on their sails, boards and clothing. The racing is a pentathlon, consisting of: triangle racing; a long distance race; freestyle; ins-and-outs; and slalom. It is open to any type of board or rig with no limits on specification, and for the competitors there are cash prizes all down the line.

There are few top sailors who appear to have any inhibitions about appearing in these events, when the only possible threat could be a ban on Olympic competition.

As there is only one entrant from each country for the Olympics, the sensible course seems to be to take the money and stop worrying, and professional events are now becoming established in Europe, the USA, and Japan.

Speed Sailing

The RYA first organized 'Speed Trials' in England in the early 1970s. They chose the enclosed Portland Harbour near Weymouth on the South Coast, running their event for one week each year in October, when in theory the wind should blow hardest.

The aim of these trials is to be the fastest sailing craft over a timed run of 500 metres – they set a circle of buoys with a 500 metre diameter which the craft can enter at any

The first British professional event was the Bacardi Isle of Man World Cup, held in 1981.

angle, so long as they pass the correct side of a centre buoy and go the full distance.

This event was never intended for boards, but by 1980 they were dominating it. In 1977 Derk Thijs has sailed a standard, but very light Windglider to 17.1 knots, and in 1979 Clive Colenso raised this to 19.2, sailing an Olympic Gold in 40 knots of wind.

By this time other countries were organizing their own Speed Trials, in part due to frustration with the Weymouth weather. Hoyle Schweitzer set up his own *Maalaea Speed Trials* on the Hawaiian island of Maui in 1980, allowing the Dutchman Jaap van der Rest to push the record to 24.45 knots.

The Boards

As speed trials have become more popular for windsurfers, the boards they use have become even simpler. In 1979 and 1980, van der Rest was running on a very short seven kg board with a single skeg, but all ideas on design and construction were thrown into confusion at Weymouth in 1981 when the German sailor Jürgen Honsheid ran at 24.75 knots on a standard surfboard with a windsurfer rig. It measured 228 cm, weighed five kg, and had around 26 litres volume – not even enough to support Honsheid's weight.

Van der Rest immediately set to work and produced his own very similar three metre surfboard pushing the record to 25.13 knots a month later at the 1981 *Pall Mall Speed Trails* in Zeera, Holland.

This makes van der Rest's board the second fastest sailing craft in the world! The fastest is the 65 foot British proa (narrow hull plus outrigger) Crossbow which ran at 36.04 in Weymouth back in 1980.

The surfboard style of board held by Englishman Mike Todd. Very difficult to sail, it evolved in Hawaii.

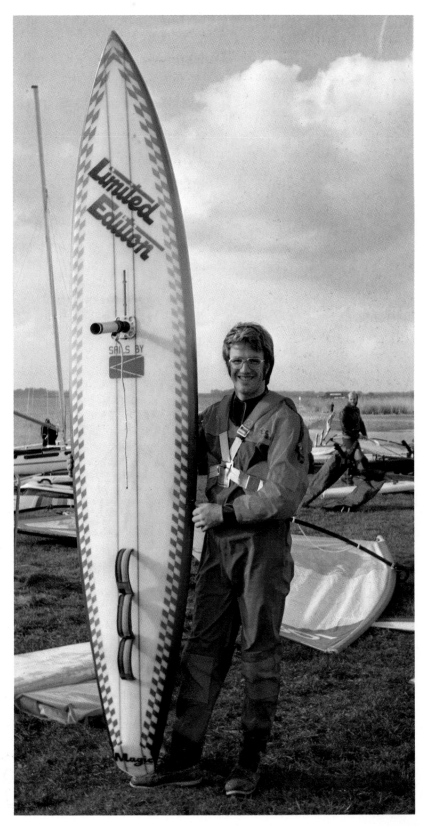

Wave Jumping

Wave jumping got started on the simple premise that if you sail fast at a wave which is also coming fast towards you, you will take off.

If the board is light and your technique is good, you will do so consistently, a fact first hit upon by the Hawaiian windsurfers who did so much to popularize and romanticize this aspect of the sport.

The great originators were Larry Stanley and Mike Horgan, who hit on the idea of a harness to reduce the strain on your arms, and footstraps to keep you and the board together.

By 1978 they had convinced Hoyle Schweitzer that he should produce a strong wind version of the Windsurfer. The resulting board was called the Rocket. They moved the daggerboard well and mast foot aft; put two skegs in place of one; gave the bow some more rocker for the waves; and bolted on footstraps.

The Rocket was the first production wave jumping board. The Hawaiians continued to lead the way with development, building one-off custom prototypes for their own use, which were snapped up by Europeans eager to try the Hawaiian experience. The most successful sailors could sell their expertise to the European volume manufacturers who were clamouring to add wave-jumping boards to their ranges – Larry Stanley designs for Alpha; Rick Naish for Mistral; and Brian Hinde and Jürgen Honsheid (German, but as good as Hawaiian) for the F2 range.

Why Hawaii?
Wave jumping boards are totally unrestricted by rules, and the Hawaiian weather (hopefully, though not always) provides constant Trade Winds of Force 4 and more in a balmy climate, which means that the sailors can try out new boards, equipment, and techniques every day. The Pacific waves come in on a 1000 mile reach, breaking on the coral heads to provide ideal waves for jumping – altogether the conditions can never be bettered in Europe, which experiences both cold winters and far less predictable wind patterns.

Therefore the Hawaiians will remain at the forefront of strong wind board development, and Europeans who feel frustrated by this fact simply solve the problem by going out and joining them.

Developments
The design and construction requirements of strong wind boards are similar, whether the boards are for wave jumping, wave riding, speed sailing, or Pan Am style racing. Conditions are rough, so the boards and their rigs must be easy to handle, and robust enough to withstand speed and waves.

Since the Windsurfer Rocket, boards used for fun in strong winds have become shorter, simpler and lighter.

With development led by Jürgen Honsheid, the fashionable board of 1980 measured around 300 cm, weighing about 12 kg, with just three or four skegs to keep it on course.

By the following year this concept had been replaced by the single skeg surfboard of the style used by Honsheid in the *Weymouth Speed Trials*. Rather than tacking, it has to be power gybed, being kept permanently on the plane to prevent it from sinking beneath the sailor's weight, which puts it rather beyond the ability of the average (or even well above average) windsurfer.

Looping the loop! Wave jumping has become sophisticated enough for experts to take part in wave jumping competitions such as the Maui Grand Prix in Hawaii.

The Pan Am Cup

The Pan Am Cup is the most prestigious event in the windsurfing calendar, with its entries booked up months in advance.

Sailed off Kailua beach on the North coast of the main Hawaiian island of Oahu, it features three main competitions leading to the overall prize: triangle racing with the emphasis on reaches rather than beats or runs; a long distance race of over 20 miles; and ins-and-outs.

None of these competitions can be held in less than Force 4, and this makes the Pan Am Cup unique. The sea boils, and the fleet is sent way out into the Pacific rollers, passing through surf breaking over coral reefs – the only saving grace is that with warm water and an onshore wind, sailors who can't handle it generally get back ashore in one piece.

The Boards

The Pan Am field is divided into *Open* and *Construction* classes. Open is sailed to IYRU Division 2 rules, but allows footstraps, while Construction means 'anything goes'.

However, apart from weight (the Construction class boards may weigh as little as 12 kg as against the Open class 18 kg) the two are very similar. Boards measure around 360 cm, and are reasonably flat for easy handling. They have big skegs and fully retracting full-length daggerboards, and are built to be as stiff and strong as possible in order to survive the pounding they get on landing after inadvertently (and frequently) taking off.

The field is dominated by boards built especially for the event. For a couple of months before it starts in late March, Hawaiians and expatriate Europeans work overtime shaping foam blocks and covering them in glassfibre, Kevlar, or something even more exotic, either for themselves or for the visitors who will buy them at inflated rates.

The next year some of these boards reappear, having been mass-produced on European production lines – the Mistral Naish, Alpha Rocket, and F2 were all developed from the Pan Am Cup.

The Winners

The winners of the Pan Am Cup are the stars of windsurfing.

Hawaiian superstar Robbie Naish (winner of the Windsurfer World Championship at the age of 13) regularly dominates it on boards built by his father Rick, with challenges from fellow American Ken Winner and West German Jürgen Honsheid, both of whom design and build their own boards, and have sailed in the Pan Am Cup since the first event in 1978 – to win it remains the highest accolade in windsurfing.

Good and Bad Years

Everyone rates the Pan Am Cup as Number One, but unfortunately it does have on-years and off-years.

1980 was the year by which all others have been judged. The wind was seldom less than Force 6, and often steadied out at around Force 8 with huge rolling seas. As a result, 170 entrants turned up the next year to be greeted by flat calm weather, so that the whole event had to be crammed into a few windy days.

They all said 1982 would be back to normal, but it was even worse. The event had to be decided on three qualifying races alone, as there wasn't enough wind for the long distance race or ins-and-outs.

However, no windsurfer is less than an optimist. They're all waiting for another year like 1980.

Bird Island, the gybe mark of the Long Distance Race in the Pan Am Cup. A fall will sweep sailor and board on to the jagged coral.

Tandems

Every windsurfer should try a tandem at least once. They're great fun, and it makes a real change to have someone else on the board enjoying themself with you.

It used to be claimed that they were also faster than one-man boards. This is certainly no longer the case as they are far too heavy, but they make up for it with an impression of speed.

Production Tandems

A limited number of manufacturers have tandems in production. Well known marques include Windglider (the most popular), Shark and Sailboard in Germany, and Flysurf in France.

The typical tandem is a lengthened, strengthened board of the usual flatboard design. It will be around 650 cm long, and will weigh about 60 kg with as much as 600 litres volume. The skin material is normally glassfibre, due to the limited production runs of these boards.

Most tandems have a very large single daggerboard, with a skeg at the stern. They have mast foot wells fore and aft, and a third well just forward of the daggerboard case. This can be used if you wish to sail your tandem singlehanded, or alternatively try it with three rigs, three-up. (This just about works if the wind is light.)

Disadvantages

The disadvantages of tandems are weight, price, and stowage.

Due to their rarity they are often more than twice the price of a conventional board, and you can't carry one on a regular saloon car roof, or keep it in a small garage. You also have to be sure you can find someone to sail the board with.

The German Shark company solved some of these problems with their Sharksurfer, which can be dismantled into short separate sections. The bow and nose sections are both about one metre long, with a slightly longer centre section to make them up into a windsurfer that stows away in a suitcase. With the alternative three metre centre section you can make it up into a tandem.

Technique

First of all, you need to decide who is captain, and sail as a team. The forward sailor backwinds the aft sailor, so he must take care not to sheet in too tight or the aft sailor will fall in. Sailing upwind, the aft sailor will sheet to the centreline with his rig raked forward, while the forward sailor sails with his rig more free, and rakes it a little aft – the Centre of Effort is somewhere between the two.

On the reach, the aft sailor will always heel his rig more than his companion – you'll have to work out whether the board goes faster with the lighter or heavier sailor in the forward position.

When running you can goosewing with one rig on either side, making the tandem particularly efficient on this point of sailing.

The procedure for tacking is started by the aft sailor and completed by the forward sailor – when gybing it's the other way around.

Above: The Windglider tandem is the original and most popular. This is a 'special' using Windglider rigs. Racing these boards is an art in itself with an enthusiastic following.

Right: The Carlsberg tandem developed from Mike Todd's *Sweeny* for the 1981 Weymouth Speed Trials (see page 126). It wasn't very fast but it provided good publicity for the sponsor.

Starting Windsurfing

There are numerous clubs and class associations you can join once you become involved in windsurfing. Whether you want to race, or simply exchange information and possibly equipment, there are organizations run by enthusiasts and professionals on a local or national basis.

Getting Started

You will benefit from joining one of these organizations before you have even stepped on a board. They will be able to provide the information on where and how to learn, and what equipment to buy. If you haven't already learnt the basics through hiring a board on the beach, or being coached by a friend, they will also be able to advise you on taking a course with a properly trained instructor.

Teaching Courses

Unless you have a genius's ability to pick up the sport, a proper teaching course will save you a lot of wasted time, and implant good techniques for your future sailing.

It is wise to go to a properly recognized school, which in most cases will be sanctioned by your national sailing authority (see Glossary). For instance, in the UK the Royal Yachting Association (RYA) is the national sailing authority with its own Boardsailing Committee, which runs a teaching scheme for windsurfers based on IWS guidelines.

IWS

International Windsurfer Schools were founded by Dagobart Benz, a former member of the German Olympic Star team. He evolved a structured teaching system which has been the foundation of the sport's success in Europe.

First steps on a Windsurfer. A small sail, not too much wind, and a warm climate make all the difference when getting started.

Benz owned a hotel in Germany, on Lake Constance, and having mastered windsurfing himself in the very early days, realized that his guests would need proper instruction to get the same enjoyment.

He therefore developed a step-by-step system of teaching, and went on to set up IWS schools all over Europe – you can recognize them by their orange flag with a black Windsurfer logo.

He trained supervizing instructors to ensure that exactly the same format was followed, using the same syllabus and issuing the same certificates. They then went back to their own countries to instruct yet more instructors, enabling the pyramid to grow and grow.

Having qualified as basic instructors, the next step was for them to gain practical teaching experience, before returning to attend a re-assessment course leading to a full instructor's licence. This re-assessment remains, and serves the dual purpose of keeping instructors up-to-date with the latest teaching techniques and maintaining high standards in the schools – principals are required to hold a full licence which must be reapplied for and renewed every two years.

Other Courses

The IWS system ensures worldwide high quality teaching, and is either followed verbatim or adapted by the relevant national authorities in all windsurfing countries.

For instance, in the UK, the RYA takes it that much further. They require an instructor to do the following: pass his instructor's course; pass an open sea test designed to ensure competent board handling in open sea conditions; hold a valid first aid certificate.

Like the IWS, RYA schools must: have a qualified instructor; provide wetsuits and buoyancy aids for their pupils; have proper changing and teaching facilities; and have a powered rescue craft on hand.

Duration

An IWS course is designed to last a full day of around eight hours. Many beginners find it easier to spread this over two or three sessions, and the schools are normally willing to make allowances.

If the weather is unsuitable (generally too much wind), you can expect to be asked back on another day at no extra charge. The overall cost will of course reflect the facilities on offer – some will be notably more luxurious and comprehensive than others.

Necessary Equipment

The school provides the board: it also provides the wetsuits (though you won't need these if you are lucky enough to be learning in the tropics).

It is up to you to find out if they provide food and refreshment or accommodation. You should normally expect to take your own towel, bathing costume, and a pair of soft rubber-soled shoes. Bare feet may grip well enough on a board, but at first you will probably find shoes are better, and that they help to protect your feet.

Format of a Course

The order and timing of a course will depend on the instructor's personal preference, coupled with weather and tidal considerations.

The order of the items may vary, but you should always expect to come across the following:

1. Introduction and simulator
You may have paid a deposit, the full amount, or you may be expected to pay on arrival.

You then get shown around and introduced to your fellow pupils (never more than eight per instructor – the fewer the better), before running through the basic parts of a sailboard, and being introduced to the dry land simulator.

This is a board mounted on a pivoted turntable (or more often the central section of an old board that has come to the end of its life afloat).

It enables you to learn the basic techniques of windsurfing without moving from a fixed spot, and without falling in and getting wet. This technique greatly cuts down teaching time, as you are not being blown away from your instructor, and are not preoccupied by being cold and wet.

You are shown how to get on the board, which will be less stable than one on the water; how to raise the rig ready for sailing; how to turn the board, sail it, steer it, and tack and gybe.

The instructor will demonstrate all these manoeuvres, and then each member of the class will be required to run through them, noting and learning by one another's mistakes.

Finally, having finished with the simulator, you will be shown how to assemble and stow the rig, as well as very important self-help techniques.

2. Tethered boards

The idea of being on a tethered board is that you can get your balance, pull the rig out of the water, and attempt to get going without being blown away by the wind or swept off by the tide – your board is tied to an anchor like a dog on a leash.

The movements you practise will be the same as those on the simulator, but the difference is that you will be falling into the water every few seconds.

Unless you are exceptionally hardy, this makes it worth ensuring that you choose a time of year when the weather is reasonably warm. This will be a far greater worry than feeling silly when you can't stay on the board – the great thing about learning in a class is that everyone else experiences exactly the same problems.

3. Group sailing

After the tethered board you can try sailing off untethered, and it's immensely rewarding when you first sail along for half a minute without falling in – every windsurfer remembers this first achievement.

As well as sailing in a straight line, you must get back to where you came from. You will have to steer the board, turn it round, and then sail it upwind, until you can sail a small triangle by the end of the course.

Weather permitting this should be possible, and so long as you don't get cold or exhausted (the two are synonymous) intervals between falls should get longer and longer.

4. Theory and detailed rigging

This is a vital part of the course, even if it takes considerably less

The simulator can be little more than a plank of wood on a turntable, with a windsurfer rig.

Alternatively it can be a full board, but either way it is as difficult as standing on a board in choppy water. The difference is that when you fall off you don't get wet and cold, and spend minutes getting back on – you simply step down on to the ground.

The pupils practice pulling up the rig, turning the board beneath the feet, and simulate sailing. Each one is criticized, but there's no need to get embarrassed – you learn from each other's mistakes. After the simulator you can get out on the water where conditions are likely to be very different. The simulator is used throughout the world – by any school that uses an IWS based teaching system.

time than practise on a simulator or afloat.

Most newcomers to windsurfing have no experience of the sea and its behaviour, and they must learn the basic laws of safety, seamanship, and courtesy afloat. Even experienced yachtsmen have to learn to tell the differences – for what is safety to them may be danger to a windsurfer.

Finally, the theory of why a sailboard does what it does must be mastered before you can control your board properly.

5. Final assessment

The instructor will decide whether you have accomplished enough to be issued with a basic certificate of competence – in some countries you are required to present this before you can hire a board or take to the water.

The majority will pass first time, and depending on the school there may be some questions on theory or a sailing trial, but nothing very onerous. Those that don't pass can come back for a further session.

Results

By the end of an IWS based course you should be able to sail a board in light winds where you choose with a small rig. You should know how to rig it and pack it all up, and you

A typical class learning the IWS system – it's the way thousands of windsurfers learn the sport each year.

should have the necessary knowledge to make the sport a safe one.

Going it Alone

If you're a lone wolf and would rather go it alone, you can teach yourself to windsurf to a basic proficiency standard from the section in this book between pages 52 and 75.

After that, stronger wind sailing and the more advanced techniques follow.

Buying a Board

The sport of windsurfing has grown so rapidly that for the manufacturers it has become like the fashion industry. Each year they introduce new models and complete new ranges, and though these may be partly justified by developments in design and manufacture, they will owe more to the strategies of the marketing men who want to keep their particular company in the forefront.

This is both good and bad when it comes to buying a board. On the one hand it guarantees that there will always be plenty of excellent buys available secondhand; on the other, if you want the latest and most up-to-the-minute creation, you must take care that it won't lose most of its value as soon as it's superseded by the next development.

The Major Marques
The ranges of most of the major manufacturers cover the five categories of boards listed on pages 18 and 19:
1. The all round/flatboard
2. The Pan Am style board
3. The Open Class roundboard
4. The wave jumping funboard
5. The extreme strong wind board

The first time buyer should always consider the first category as the one to go for, and within it he is unlikely to make a bad buy so long as he sticks to a well-known brand of board.

The Windsurfer Regatta or Mistral Competition, for instance, are first time buyers' boards *par excellence* – they have been established for years; continue to be very good to sail; have enthusiastic one-design followings; and are consequently widely sought after.

The alternative may be a flatboard that has been set up for strong wind sailing, usually with footstraps and the provision for a storm daggerboard. It will probably be frustratingly slow to sail in light winds, but so long as it comes from a relatively well-known manufacturer will be a safe buy.

Remember that the major manufacturers compete directly on price and quality, and cannot afford to get the construction or design of a board wrong when they are tooling up for minimum runs of thousands of units. Even if they do change models each season, the new ones are developed from successions of prototypes which guarantee that the end products are reliable.

Price Differentials
The world market is dominated by a handful of manufacturers from Germany, France and the Netherlands.

Ninety per cent of their market is dominated by the first time buyers' or all-round style board, and since they are all producing a very similar product, there is scant allowance for variation in price.

Some boards are very cheap, while others aim to have the kudos of being the best. For instance, the Mistral Competition may be twice the price of the Dufour Sun. It will be equipped to much the same specification and perform in much the same way, but it has the 'name' to sell at a far higher price, and continue to hold that price in the secondhand market.

Boards and Rigs
Most boards are sold complete with rig. However, rigs are interchangeable from board to board, and when you progress to owning three or more boards, you will begin to buy rigs and boards separately.

For the first-time buyer it is best to stick with the rig recommended by the manufacturer. This will seldom be the height of sophistication, but when you don't have the experience to tell the difference, it hardly matters.

You will probably have the option of different sail sizes. Again, which one you choose doesn't matter much in the long term. As you progress through the sport you will find that you need at least three different sails to cope with varying wind conditions.

The illustrations on pages 80–81 show a typical range offered by a sailmaker. An average beginner wants a sail that is easy to handle; say 4.8 square metres for someone who is relatively small; 5.6 sq m for someone of average strength; and a full 6.5 sq m for a six footer who is fit and young.

Choose which sail suits your physical capabilities best when starting to windsurf; then add more sails as you improve your technique.

Ancillaries
Getting equipped for windsurfing can involve spending a lot of money. You will need:
A car – unless you can borrow one. (A Suzuki jeep has just the right image.)
A roof rack – if this doesn't have a lock, it may be worth investing in a board lock to prevent your windsurfer being stolen.
Insurance – against the board being stolen, unfortunately an increasingly popular pastime. This will also help pay for broken masts and boards.
A wetsuit
Boots
Gloves
A dry suit – *de rigeur* in cold water.
A harness
You will of course also need the *board* (or boards), and a *rig* (or rigs) with several *sails*. Thankfully you won't have to buy the whole lot at once, and you can always save money by borrowing equipment, or buying some of it secondhand.

Other needs include *spare parts*

This showroom at Chelsea Wharf Windsurfing in London has plenty of different boards, and with thousands more available secondhand, the choice becomes even more bewildering.

(the mast foot breaks every now and then), *tools* (at least a knife and a screwdriver), a *repair kit*, various bits of *spare line*, and possibly some *certificates*.

The necessity for the certificates varies from country to country, and from place to place. To hire a board, race it, or just to take your own on a certain piece of water may require an official-looking piece of paper. Enquire before you go – your national sailing authority may be a good source of information, and in the UK the RYA will issue you with a Certificate of Competence for a modest fee.

In other circumstances you may have to prove your worth, and an IWS Certificate given to those who successfully pass their learners' course is normally fairly useful.

The Elements
The board
Made from plastic, there should be no bumps, hollows, or cracks. The join along the sides should appear perfect. There should be a good non-slip finish on deck, but be wary of hard angles – odd-shaped decks tend to be cosmetic rather than functional.

The hull should be completely foam filled. Check that there is enough buoyancy to carry your weight – at least 230 litres for 10 stone.
The skeg
Plastic
The daggerboard
Plastic, and for ease of use retracting flush with the hull. Laminated ply daggerboards tend to be used for racing – they are more efficient and lighter, but require more care.
Skeg boxes, daggerboard cases, and mast foot wells
Either integral with the moulding of the board, or separate plastic units bonded into position. Often one specialist manufacturer supplies the same units for several different boards, so they are interchangeable.

Universal joint
Usually plastic and nylon. Attached to the mast foot which is the 'adaptor' that enables you to change rigs from board to board. It must have the facility to leash the rig to the board.
The mast
Usually glassfibre made on the same principle as fishing rods. Tapered alloy extrusions are used for racing, but are more likely to suffer damage.
The wishbone
Rubber sleeved alloy with plastic end fittings. The less flex the better.
The sail
Terylene. Quality of cloth and cut vary considerably.

Where to Buy
A specialist dealer with a wind-surfing school attached to his shop should be able to give advice, and provide a full service back-up including warranty work, repairs, replacements, and trade-ins (most dealers will now take boards in part exchange as their customers trade up).

However you may prefer to explore the secondhand market. Either way, remember the following rules:

* *The latest in regatta or jump boards may be very expensive when new. As soon as it is superseded, its value will plummet.*
* *Better to stick with a board that is still in production (the longer the better) and selling well. It will always hold its price.*
* *A board made from a tough material will hold its value well.*
* *Boards break up. If the foam inside a board begins to delaminate, restoration will be expensive – you would have done better to have spent more in the first place.*
* *Check the equipment that is being sold with the board. Rigs are expensive, and there is a great difference between a good regatta sail and an allweather sail that is too small.*

Most shops have a wide range of boards and accessories, and are run by staff who are enthusiasts. This normally means that their advice can be relied upon when you don't know what to buy. Unless you are very sure of your ground, always go for a well known brand, and if possible seek advice on it. There have been few horrors from the major manufacturers in the last few years, though it's true that some boards are not quite as good as others.

Right: The major Open Class racing championships are treated by the manufacturers as showcases for their marques, even though they frequently race one-off prototypes dressed up to look like production boards so you can't tell the difference.

Care and Repair

A board that is misused will deteriorate rapidly, particularly if the construction is fragile. If you are the sort of person who enjoys messing about doing minor repairs, well and good, but if you'd rather never lift a finger, think twice about that board with the ultra-thin gel coat.

General Upkeep
Cleaning the board
Try a proprietary domestic cleaner. If there is any tar on the board, go over it with white spirit first.
Storing the board
Boards can warp. Always store your board with support along its full length.
Sails
'Flake' the sail with parallel folds along the luff and leech. Alternatively roll it around the luff.

Give the sail a bath. Leave it overnight in warm water containing detergent. If there are any stains in the morning, give it a scrub, and then rinse in fresh water.

Tar can be dealt with by carbon tetrachloride or petrol, but always check colour fastness before you get carried away.

Repairs
Minor repairs to the board, such as scratches and cracks can be dealt with by the amateur. Major repairs are best left to the professional, who has the right equipment and the experience of having done the job before. It is not necessarily difficult, but on your first attempt you stand a good chance of making a mess, so if it's a new board leave it alone.

The major materials all have different properties when it comes to repairs.
Polyethylene
Can be welded using a soldering iron, a Stanley knife, and poly-

Above: The repair and modification of old polyethylene boards has become a fine art. One way of replacing soggy foam is to cut it out, patch the area over, and then pour in liquid foam.

Below: The foam expands and solidifies, and the excess can be scraped off with a sharp knife. It is unlikely to be a very beautiful repair, but it should be effective and rejuvenate the board.

Left: Gluing the rubber cap back on to the end of the wishbone. This is one of many simple repairs that can normally be undertaken by the owner.

However, unless you're a do-it-yourself enthusiast, major repairs are best left to specialists. Most windsurfing shops have someone who is experienced in dealing with polyethylene boards, and can turn his hand to GRP or ABS at reasonable cost.

A soldering iron can be used for welding polyethylene or plastic rod, which can then be trimmed with a sharp knife. Alternatively, the plastic rod can be fed through a 'hot gun' which has different sized nozzles, and is more accurate.

Above: Taking a saw to an old Windsurfer to turn it into a strong wind home-made Rocket used to be a popular pastime.

ethylene rod. Cross-linked poly-ethylene has the reputation of being very difficult to deal with – if you're unsure leave it to a specialist who can use a proper heat welding gun.

ABS

Cracks can be filled using a solvent paste which dissolves the surrounding plastic. This can also be used for applying ABS patches, and is part of a suitable repair kit sold by the Dufour marque.

ASA

Has a tendency to discolour when subjected to amateur repair, and is safer left to the professional.

Glassfibre

Theoretically the easiest material to repair. Bits of missing gel coat can be re-gelled, and glass mat added for extensive repairs.

Repairs with epoxy resin should not be undertaken by the amateur.

Foaming

The central core of most boards is the foam. If this needs replacing, a section can be cut out so that it can be re-foamed. This does not apply to polystyrene foam.

Major Damage

The most common breakages are masts and daggerboards. Glassfibre masts can be repaired, while daggerboards are relatively cheap to replace.

Board damage is sometimes the result of structural deterioration when the board has been incorrectly foamed. The faulty foam must be replaced.

Fibreglass masts are very prone to damage. You normally get a clean break at the wishbone, and this can be repaired using a 'sleeve', for which you can use a section of an old mast (above). Glue it inside or outside with epoxy resin, and then wrap fibreglass 'ape around it.

It is wise to reinforce your mast at the base, wishbone attachment, and tip, by wrapping round fibreglass tape treated with epoxy resin. This won't affect the flexibility of the mast.

The base of the mast is liable to splinter, but it can be bound with synthetic thread.

Windsurfing Accessories

Windsurfing is big business for manufacturers and retailers. As far as they're concerned, once you get started you don't just buy a board and leave it at that.

They want you to come back and buy a strong wind board and a racing board, and to keep on trading them in for newer, better models each season. They also expect you to be suitably dressed, with the flashiest of wetsuits for windsurfing, and the very minimum of a Hawaiian T-shirt for après-windsurfing.

Apart from the clothing and the boards, they would also like you to spend your money on every kind of hardware.

Is It Worth It?

You should never forget that the manufacturers and the retailers are there to make money, and you should therefore treat their products with a certain amount of caution. As with many other sports only a few items of equipment are absolutely vital.

What You Really Need

On the following pages we shall run through the items you really need, for yourself and the board.

Proper clothing is very important and should be carefully chosen. Unfortunately price does tend to reflect quality, although there are short cuts. If your budget is limited, you can make a very acceptable wetsuit from a kit, using the offcuts for neoprene socks which you can wear with oversize tennis shoes. You won't be the best dressed windsurfer, but you can still overtake him in a flurry of spray.

You could also overtake him wearing secondhand gear, for as accessories are restyled and revamped for each new season, so the trendiest windsurfers sell off their gear to keep abreast of the times. It's lucky that most clothing is made to a high standard, and will

be good for several more years after a solitary season's use.

Proper accessories for your person include wetsuit, footwear, gloves, and eventually a harness. You may wish to add a buoyancy aid, and if it's cold you should also add a dry suit.

Proper accessories for your board amount to a roof rack, some straps to tie the board and rig to it, a lock, and possibly a trolley.

However if you feel you want more, there are plenty more accessories of varying usefulness.

Bags

You can get bags for your board, rig, and daggerboard.

A bag for your board is useful if the board is fragile, or perhaps you feel it might fade in the sun?

A bag for your rig is very useful. There are two types, of which Type 2 is the better. Both are long sausages with room to slide in the mast with the sail wrapped tightly around it. However Type 2 has a cut-out and zips along its length, so that you can leave the wishbone attached to the mast during the whole operation. You can then lash it alongside.

Both Types 1 and 2 should be rain resistant and have a pocket in which to stow the battens.

A bag for your daggerboard is only useful if the daggerboard is very fragile – ie an expensive laminated wooden job for racing. Then it should preferably be heavily quilted.

You can also have a personal bag to carry all your odds and ends. The yachtsman's soft carry-all is recommended – the best ones have separate sections for wet clothing and pockets for tools, tape, etc.

Strong Wind Sailing

Strong wind sailing accessories are endless. Apart from half a dozen sails and three wishbones, there is:

A storm daggerboard
A short daggerboard that won't

aquaplane and makes strong wind sailing considerably easier.

Well worth buying if it's offered with the board you sail.

Footstraps
More and more new boards have the option of footstraps which can be left on or off. They're well worth considering, as once again they make the board much easier to sail in strong winds.

If the board has no provision for footstraps you can buy footstrap kits. However, unless you're good at do-it-yourself this job may need to be done by a professional. The alternative is to stick on strips of seat-belt webbing with fibreglass, which can look a trifle messy.

Skegs
As the wind gets stronger, the board becomes more inclined to luff and less inclined to travel in a straight line. You can solve the first problem with a storm daggerboard and the second with bigger skegs. These come in a variety of shapes and sizes, with unlikely names that reflect their shapes: *Donkey's Ear*, *Noserider*, and *Kanger's Cock*. (The latter predictably originated from Australia.)

They all have two things in common – they are all expensive, and easily broken. Also, their efficiency seems to vary according to the board and the person on it.

A strong wind specialist who knows exactly what he wants will probably benefit from the more rarefied skegs. Unless you come into that category, you will almost certainly do better to stick with the skegs provided by the manufacturer.

Hawaiian uphaul
An elasticated uphaul line that has no need of shockcord to leash it to the mast foot since it's under tension all the time. Nor does it need granny knots as handholds since it's so thick and squidgy.

Racing daggerboards are made of sheets of laminated plywood.

Clothing

You should never underestimate how debilitating cold water is, and unless you live in the tropics, you should always dress sensibly and correctly when you go windsurfing.

Wetsuit

A wetsuit is a tight fitting neoprene suit three or four mm thick. The fine layer of water between the neoprene and your body is the insulation which keeps you warm.

To work properly, the suit must be tight, but windsurfing is a strenuous sport and the suit should be flexible enough not to constrict movement. Most important of all, you should not wear tight sleeves which will constrict the muscles of the forearms and lead to cramp.

The ideal windsurfing wetsuit is a 'long john' with ankle zips. On top you can wear a windproof nylon jacket, or a wetsuit bolero with loose sleeves that allow the water to drain if you fall in.

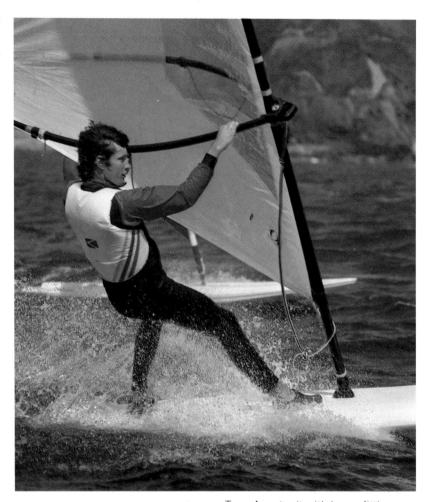

Top: A wetsuit with loose fitting sleeves does not constrict the sailor's arms, which would suffer from cramp in a tight fitting suit. However, it is important that the water drains from the sleeves when you fall in, or swimming becomes very difficult. Here Dee Caldwell wears shoes, and a harness with full support for his back.

Above: Three types of suits. The Long John is easier to put on with ankle zips, while the two 'shorties' are for warmer weather.

Above: You can wear mittens or gloves, but the palm should be reinforced for the wishbone.

Right: A simple windsurfing shoe and an expensive boot. It is the rubber compound that grips the board – not the tread.

Dry suits are expensive, but you should be sure to buy a good quality brand – it will give years of service.

Wetsuits vary from the practical to the ultra chic, but it's simple black neoprene rubber that keeps you warm!

The neoprene is warmer and dries faster if it is unlined, but is more prone to tearing and damage. It is therefore preferable to have it lined with nylon or Lycra, and for windsurfing use it must have kneepads for when you climb back on the board.

Good suits are very expensive, but you can set to work with a neoprene wetsuit kit for a much smaller outlay. It won't look as good, but it serves the same purpose.

Boots

Some boards have a good bare foot non-slip surface, but most do not. For the learner it may be preferable to wear shoes regardless, to avoid bruising inexperienced feet.

You must find the right rubber sole compound to suit the surface of the board. Tennis shoes are fine on some, and useless on others. Alternatively you can get properly designed windsurfing shoes and boots. All have one thing in common – they are extraordinarily expensive.

Gloves

Not really necessary in the summer, when you should put up with hardening your hands.

In cold winter, neoprene mittens seem the most effective answer. They should be shaped like a fist clenched over the wishbone, with a heavily reinforced palm.

Headgear

The crotch and the cranium are the two greatest areas of heat loss on the human body. In cold weather protect the head with a neoprene skull cap.

Dry suit

The dry suit is made of proofed nylon material designed to keep the water out. You can get into it wearing your clothes, or more sensibly in a suit of thermal underwear, fall in the water and stay completely dry.

It has a heavy duty waterproof zip, and tight rubber seals at the neck and wrists which must be a good enough fit to be comfortable, while keeping the water out.

The dry suit is only suitable for

very cold weather. It doesn't breathe, and you soon get too hot inside. It is also rather bulky and cumbersome, and is almost impossible to swim in, even with all the air expelled (you do a knees bend, letting the air out through the neck when you first put it on).

Buoyancy

Few windsurfers seem to wear buoyancy aids – they don't think the image is right!

This is nonsense. A buoyancy vest won't constrict your movements, and when you fall into the water for the umpteenth time and suddenly discover you are very tired, you will be glad of it.

Don't take any notice of the claims for buoyancy possessed by wetsuits – it's not sufficient to keep you afloat without worrying. (Wearing a dry suit is like swimming in the Dead Sea, but be careful not to invert with all the air around your feet!)

The most sensible answer may be to go for a harness with integral buoyancy (see pages 92–93) though remember the buoyancy is only equivalent to an *aid*, and is not a *lifejacket* – if you're knocked out it may float you on your face.

Carrying a Board

A board can be carried on a car roof, using a specially designed gutter rack.

This will take a couple of boards and their rigs side by side. The best way to tie them down is with webbing straps that lock on sprung teeth. The strap passes over the board, under the rack, back again, under the rack, and locks through itself. You should take an extra turn around the mast which is placed along the centreline of the board, together with the wishbone.

You can carry as many as four or five boards, but then it is better to

Top: Special board straps should be used with a roofrack. Rope is not nearly as effective and may damage the board. Remember to tie the ends of the straps, and tighten the roofrack.

There are various ways of carrying a board down to the beach, the worst of which is carrying it under your arm. Patent trolley systems are designed to take the board, rig, and your gear (above and below) but you should ensure that the wheels are big enough to cope with soft sand. It is best if you can lash your gear securely to the trolley or it will tend to come adrift, particularly with the simplest types of trolley (below right).

Top: A clever idea from the Hi Fly range. Little wheels slot in to the skeg boxes.

Without a trolley you must carry the board with one hand in the daggerboard case (below). You can then lash the wishbone alongside. Hopefully production boards will get lighter and lighter in years to come – fairly soon we should expect them to weigh little more than 10 kg. A shoulder strap (above) with slings that pass under the board makes life a little easier, and was copied from the surfers. On a windy day you have to take care that you don't get whirled around like a weathercock. Carrying the board over your head (right) may solve the problem, but soon gets tiring.

tie them with shockcord to let them have some 'give'. With such a load you should accelerate, brake, and corner very gingerly.

With a very short car it may be wise to tie down either end of the board(s) to the bumpers. You can use the towing eye and skeg.

You can buy racks with built-in locking systems, which are valuable if you feel there is a chance of the board being stolen. A cheaper alternative is a continuous loop of wire which passes through a lock. This is fed through the daggerboard case and then the two ends are locked together from both sides *inside the car*. The wire is sufficiently thin to enable you to close the car doors on it.

To the Water
Boards are surprisingly heavy. 18 kg doesn't sound much, but it's plenty to carry over half a mile – and then you have to go back and get the rig, daggerboard etc.

The best way to carry a board is under your arm with one hand in the underside of the daggerboard case, and the other in the mast foot well – it helps if it's a T-piece section. Alternatively you can carry it over your head, but that seems like an excellent way of getting exhausted before you start.

There are plenty of patent trolley systems, working around the principle of a pair of wheels on which you can push the board and rig. The trouble is that most of them get bogged down when they encounter sand – if you're going to the beach, the bigger the wheels the better. For preference, they should be shaped like footballs to keep the maximum area in contact with the sand.

If there are two of you, and two boards, the best way to maximise strength and resources is to carry the boards deck to deck, with one of you holding the bows in either hand, while the other does likewise with the sterns.

Basic Theory

The theory behind windsurfing may seem a little complicated, but it you want to succeed it is worth taking the trouble to understand it.

A sail generates drive. Some of it is forward, but a lot is sideways – this is converted into forward drive for the board by means of the daggerboard.

The drive is termed the *Centre of Effort* – a movable point on the sail which takes the main thrust of the wind's power. The daggerboard, which resists the sideways drive, is the *Centre of Lateral Resistance*.

If the Centre of Effort (CE) balances with the Centre of Lateral Resistance (CLR), the board will be in equilibrium. In this state it is designed so that it will sail in a straight line, though no designer can allow for sea conditions.

Sail Drive

When it blows on to a correctly trimmed sail, the air flow separates and passes on either side. On the leeward side (the one furthest from the wind) the air flow is accelerated by the curve which has been built into the sail. The result is a reduction in air pressure. The high pressure area on the windward side of the sail (closest to the wind) then pushes toward the low pressure, and thus generates drive.

The drive is roughly at right angles to the chord of the sail – an imaginary line drawn between the clew (where the end of the sail meets the wishbone) and the mast. Its efficiency in propelling the board will obviously depend on your course in relation to the wind:

Close hauled

Sailing towards the wind, you would expect to be pushed sideways and backwards. The aerodynamic shape of the daggerboard combats this tendency, converting movement into forward drive.

There are exceptions to this general rule. Experts can sail strong wind boards on a close hauled course with a single skeg to combat leeway (moving sideways). However speed is imperative. The board must be planing in a minimum wind strength of Force 4, and even then the sailor's technique will be critical.

Reaching

When the wind is on the beam there is less sideways drive and less pressure on the daggerboard. Consequently, this is always the fastest point of sailing.

Running

One would expect sailing with the wind behind to give the most drive. Not so – the wind is only hitting the sail on one side, and consequently there is no area of low pressure. The sail is simply pushed along rather than sucked, while the air flow round the edges suffers from turbulence.

Apparent Wind

The *apparent wind* is the wind *experienced by the sailor*, and is not the same as *true wind*, which is the wind *experienced by someone standing still*.

If a windsurfer is sailing towards a true wind of 15 knots at a board speed of five knots, he will be experiencing an apparent wind speed of nearly 20 knots. However, if he were sailing away from a true wind of 15 knots, we would need to deduct his board speed (say 5 knots) to find the strength of the apparent wind on his sail (10 knots). This is less than the true wind, and combined with no aerodynamic suck on his sail, running becomes a slow point of sailing.

The faster a board sails, the more the apparent wind will change in direction, blowing increasingly from ahead. Thus a board travelling at high speed will need to trim its sail far tighter than one travelling slowly, even though the true wind remains constant in its direction and power.

Sail Trim

The sail's drive is determined by its camber, which is the degree of fullness in the sail and its trim. To find the correct angle of attack, the sail should be trimmed so that its chord is no closer than 15–20 degrees to the apparent wind. If it is closer, the air flow will break away into turbulence to leeward, which will brake rather than suck the sail. On the other hand, if it is not sheeted in enough, all the air flow will shift to the leeward side, and the whole sail will lift and lose efficiency.

Eventually you will be able to trim the sail by instinct. You will find you also need to tune the amount of camber, which can be adjusted by tightening the outhaul and downhaul. With a bendy mast and the shape already cut into the sail, the pull on the leech and luff will change it from full to flat to suit the conditions.

Broadly speaking, a full sail is used for light breezes; a medium-full sail for moderate winds; and a flat sail for strong winds.

Board Shape

Apart from sail drive, a board's performance is also affected by several other factors. To perform to maximum advantage it must be in perfect balance. This will be determined by: the size and position of the skeg(s); the size, shape, and position of the daggerboard; the distance between the daggerboard and the skeg(s); the distance between the mast step and the stern; the design of the rig; and the design of the board.

Board shape and design is limited, and will normally be a mixture of a square, pin, or round-tail outline, allied with a bottom that is flat, triangular, trapezoid, or round.

Many factors contribute to steering the board. In addition to steering with the rig, the position of the skeg, daggerboard, and mast foot is critical.

Steering the Board

We have seen that a windsurfer is balanced by the correct design of the board and rig. The sailor keeps control by varying the relationship between the CE and CLR.

By tilting the rig forward, the CE is moved forward of the CLR. This pushes the board's nose away from the wind (ie it bears off). Conversely, by tilting the rig aft, the board's stern is pushed away from the wind (it heads up).

This basic theory behind steering a course is tempered by many factors: your board will never be in 100 percent perfect balance; the sea will affect the board's course; and a puff of wind will shift the CE further aft. You will learn that if you luff the rig (let the sail out) the board will head up, and if you sheet in it will bear away – the CE moves aft and forward respectively.

When you are running straight downwind, steering with the rig is somewhat different. The CE points directly forward, while the CLR points aft, so you tilt the rig to one side or the other rather than backwards or forwards. If you tilt it to the windward side the board will bear away; and if you tilt it to leeward it will head up.

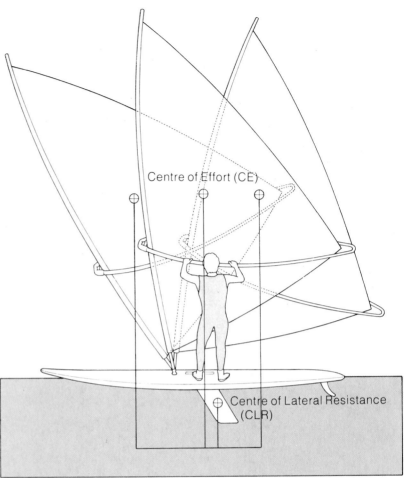

Above: The Centre of Effort is the fulcrum of the wind's force on the sail. If it is directly over the Centre of Lateral Resistance, the board will travel in a straight line. Rake the CE forward of the CLR, and it will push the nose away from the wind. Rake it aft, and it will push the stern away from the wind so that you bear up.

When the wind increases, the sailor is unable to hold the rig in the upright position. This is the point where a conventional sailcraft would begin to heel away from the wind. The boardsailor heels the rig into the wind, and hangs beneath it, with his weight supported by the pull of the sail, while his board remains flat.

The sailor hangs on to the rig with his Centre of Gravity well outboard. The push of the mast foot will make the board heel away from him, but his feet will act as a counterbalance.

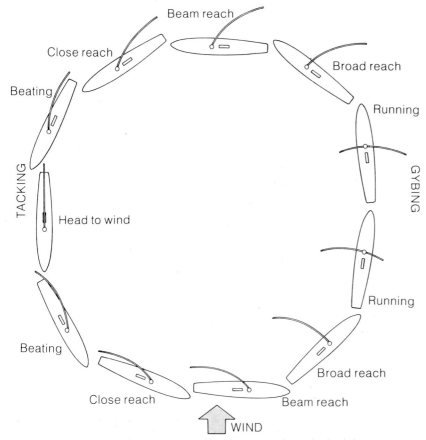

Beam reach

Close reach

Beating

Broad reach

Running

TACKING

GYBING

Head to wind

Running

Beating

Broad reach

Close reach

Beam reach

WIND

Above: The points of sailing, travelling in a complete circle. It is very necessary practice for a learner to be able to sail in any direction – not just downwind, which is easiest when you begin, and the most difficult point when you get better and take on strong winds.

Balancing the Wind

A yacht heels over as the force of the wind increases, effectively cutting down its sail area and drive. As well as losing drive, it also loses keel area (CLR) and makes greater leeway (moving sideways rather than forwards).

In the case of the windsurfer, however, it is the rig rather than the hull that is inclined, but in the direction the wind is coming from. The same drive continues, but with less projected sail area; the efficiency of the CLR continues; and at the same time the rig generates 'lift' to make the board lighter and faster.

The more it blows, the more you cant the rig to windward, with your weight hanging beneath it. It takes a lot of faith to lean back and let the rig carry you, but in anything over Force 3 it becomes essential to windsurfing.

Conclusions

Once you have mastered the principle of CE and CLR, you will realise that the remainder of board control is a compromise – between the board's design, the rig, the conditions, and your technique. Only experience can give you all the answers.

As well as the mastfoot, the motion of the long daggerboard through the water will also make the board heel away from the wind, particularly when it is blowing hard. A smaller daggerboard may help.

Course sailed

Driving force

Total force

20°

Angle of attack

Leeway force

APPARENT WIND

The chord of the sail is angled at approximately 20 degrees to get the best angle of attack: If you don't sheet in enough, the sail will blow back as the wind hits it on the leeward side – if you oversheet it, the driving force will be nothing like as effective. You will soon find the correct sheeting angle instinctively.

First Attempts

You've got the board, you understand the basics, and now you're ready to try windsurfing.

First, choose your day! The most important factors will be weather and the place you intend to sail from. If they are unsuitable, you stand a fair chance of wasting your time. Don't go out if it's freezing cold; blowing too hard or flat calm with no wind; or if there are waves breaking on the beach. Any of these factors will be enough to put you off if it's your first attempt.

Offshore Winds
The great danger for a learner on a windsurfer is being blown away from the shore. An offshore wind blowing off the land will get progressively stronger as you get further out. If you find you can't cope, you will spend more and more time falling into the water with the wind pushing you in a direction you don't want to go, at an ever-increasing speed. The end result is that you will eventually need to be rescued.

Therefore, if you're sailing on open water, always beware of an offshore wind. Near to the shore it will be broken up by obstacles, such as trees and houses, making gusty, difficult conditions; further out it may be a lot stronger than you bargained for.

However, an onshore wind may be just as unsatisfactory. The wind heaps up waves, and depending on how the shore shelves, this can easily build up into surf with a fierce undertow – conditions which can be handled by experienced sailors alone – otherwise the all too frequent results are broken masts, wishbones and daggerboards.

Even small waves will present a problem, because on your first attempts you will find the board quite unstable enough on flat calm water – and you don't want to make this any worse.

The ideal compromise is when the wind is blowing more or less parallel to the shore, and coming from a direction that is unobstructed. The wind won't be gusty and the water will be flat, and if its direction is slightly angled onshore it will blow you home in the end. If it's not, you should check that there is a lee shore (one that the wind is blowing on to) at an angle to the shore you are sailing off.

Tides
Tides are just as dangerous as offshore winds. Unless you research an area thoroughly before you sail in it, there is no way of telling if there is any tide, and where and how fast it runs. Tides frequently run at as much as four knots, and can create conditions that only a very experienced sailor can get out of.

The answer is to establish in advance whether the tide is going out or coming in (High Water is normally followed by Low Water with an interval of about six hours. It then takes another six hours to build up to High Water once again.) You should also find out if certain states of the tide are unsafe.

(You will do well to establish whether there is a two mile walk over the beach to the sea at Low Water. When you're carrying a board this will seem a long way – you'll wish you'd worked this sort of thing out before you decided to go off sailing.)

Cold
Cold is the beginner's great enemy, particularly in Northern countries.

The effect of cold water and a chilling wind can have an alarming effect on your body heat, lowering it critically before you realise what has happened. This condition, called hypothermia, is dangerous for beginners who spend a lot of time falling in the water, and then sitting on their boards getting colder and colder. As the hypothermia worsens, the victim becomes increasingly unable to cope: strength fails; reflexes slow; and willpower decreases.

For this reason it is imperative to dress correctly and sensibly. Wear a wetsuit, boots, and a windproof top on any day when there is the remotest chance of getting cold – it's better to overheat and be sensible.

Inshore Water
Inshore waters might seem most suitable to the beginner. There is always a lee shore not too far away, and so long as the piece of water is relatively small, it hardly matters if the wind is offshore from where you start off.

However, some stretches of inland water are quite large, and it doesn't take many things to go wrong before you can find yourself in serious trouble.

Unless the country is very low-lying, the wind is liable to be gusty, owing to obstructions on shore. In addition, the water may be considerably colder, and far less buoyant than seawater. A fitful wind and very cold water is a prime cause of hypothermia. (In fact the only windsurfing fatality in the UK so far occurred in just these conditions in the Lake District – and the victim was not wearing a wetsuit.)

Weather Forecasts
How do you judge if the weather will be suitable? First, you should look out for weather forecasts that are designed for yachtsmen. There are numerous shipping forecasts on the radio throughout the day, and these should always be posted up by sailing clubs. Or you can look in a newspaper or telephone a weather centre.

It really helps if your first attempts can be made on a nice sunny day with a light breeze. At first, rigging will seem complicated, but you soon find that once you can rig one board, you can rig them all in little more than five minutes.

Seamanship

Before you take to the water, you must understand the basics of seamanship, and particularly the *Rules of the Road*. Showing courtesy to others while afloat is a major safety factor.

'Rules of the Road'
The rules of the road are designed to stop boats hitting one another. They apply to tankers, yachts, speed boats, dinghies, and windsurfers – in fact anything on the water.

The rules of the road for windsurfers are internationally recognized – they're the same as the ones for yachts. They are simple to understand and not at all like the more complex rules used for racing.
1. A board on starboard tack has right of way over one on port tack.

You are on starboard tack when the wind is coming from the starboard side. If you find this difficult to remember, some wishbone coverings are green on one side (starboard) and red on the other (port – remember the colour of the drink).
2. The overtaking craft must keep clear.

(This is a matter of courtesy. However life becomes increasingly less courteous once you become involved in racing.)
3. When two craft on the same tack are converging, the one to leeward has right of way.

In effect this means that the craft sailing a higher course has right of way – if you are reaching, and the other chap is beating to windward with both of you on the same tack, you give way.

Meeting Other Craft
The above three basic rules will serve when you meet another windsurfer. In principle they should apply when you meet any type of sailing yacht.

The written exception is when the other yacht is having to negotiate a channel, and would be put aground or on the rocks if you tried to enforce your right of way. However, there are other important *unwritten* exceptions which depend on your commonsense and courtesy.
1. Craft that are racing have right of way over ones that are not.

This is because every inch counts when you're racing, and if a racer has to change course he may lose ground and places to his rivals, while for someone who's out on a jaunt it really doesn't matter.

Therefore, if it's easy for you to give way (even though he's on port and you're on starboard) you would be sensible to do so gracefully; if not, you are under no obligation to do so. (Remember that people who race sometimes get extremely aggressive and overheated, and assume they have right of way over *anything* on the water. This is most certainly not the case, and you don't automatically have to get out of the way just because someone yells 'I'm racing'.)

The rules for racing sailboats are a study in themselves. There are very many of them and they are very complex – you need a book specifically on the subject.
2. Larger craft have the right of way over smaller ones.

It is a written rule that pleasure craft give right of way to commercial craft – never try to mix it with an oil tanker!

However, your windsurfer does have the right of way over a hundred-foot schooner if you are on starboard and he is on port.

It would be patently ridiculous to insist on this. You can change course in seconds, while for the yacht it will be a major undertaking. Therefore on principle it is a sensible idea to reckon on generally giving way to all cabin craft, keel boats etc (though not if they are stupid and inconsiderate enough to barge through a windsurfer race

course). Remember that you are probably sailing the most nimble, easily manoeuvred craft on the water, and give way accordingly.
3. Others may not understand the Rules of the Road.

It pays to assume that others are not so well informed as you are, or simply don't know what course you are steering – a novice windsurfer often sails in an unpredictably variable direction. If a speedboat is heading straight at you he should certainly give way, but it would be foolish to take it for granted that he will.

Similarly, if you are steering unpredictably you can hardly expect another craft to know which way to turn in order not to foul you.
4. Don't make a nuisance of yourself on beaches or with swimmers.

Remember that dragging a rig over people's heads doesn't go down well, and a board can be extremely dangerous. Left on the beach upside down, someone is liable to trip over it, and on the water the bow or the skeg could be lethal for a swimmer, if you're careering around partly out of control.

Because of this you will find local bylaws that prohibit windsurfing in certain places, both inland and on the coast. Busy beaches have areas set aside, with windsurfing lanes to get boards away from the swimmers.

Commonsense
Both sea and inland waters can be very unfriendly to a lonely little figure on a windsurfer. So, when you first try windsurfing:
1. Check the weather.
2. Check the area.
3. Check the safety facilities.
4. Ensure someone knows what you are doing.
5. Wear the right clothing.
6. Know the rules of the road.
7. Don't bite off more than you can chew, for unintentional rescue is ignominy.

The Beaufort Scale

The wind is measured on the Beaufort Scale, invented by Admiral Beaufort in 1805. The units are knots, which are nautical miles (about 1.85 kilometres) per hour. These descriptions are for life on the open sea. It won't be quite so extreme close inshore, which is windsurfer territory, but it would be highly unusual for most people to sail effectively in Force 7 or 8.

Force 0
1 knot or less. Calm. Mirror-like sea.

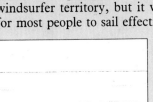

Force 1
1–3 knots. Light air. Gently scaly ripples.

Force 2
4–6 knots. Light breeze. Small wavelets. May have glassy crests but these will not break.

Force 3
7–10 knots. Gentle breeze: large wavelets. Crests begin to break. Possibly some white horses.

Force 4
11–16 knots. Moderate breeze. Waves becoming longer with white horses.

Force 5
17–21 knots. Fresh breeze. Moderate waves with white horses and possibly occasional spray.

Force 6
22–27 knots. Strong breeze. Large waves forming with extensive white crests and spray.

Force 7
28–33 knots. Near gale. Sea heaps up and foam from breaking waves blows in streaks.

Force 8
34–40 knots. Gale. Moderately high waves. Edge of crests break into spindrift. Well marked streaks.

Force 9
41–47 knots. Severe gale. High waves. Confused breaking crests. Spray affects visibility.

Force 10
48–55 knots. Storm. Very high waves with long overhanging crests. Sea surface becomes white.

Force 11
56–63 knots. Violent storm. Exceptionally high waves hiding ships from view. Sea covered in white foam.

Force 12
64 knots plus. Hurricane. Air full of driving spray. Very bad visibility.

Understanding the Weather

A windsurfer is interested in wind – as you become more proficient you'll curse the weather if there isn't enough of it!

However, you may also run into problems if there is too much wind, and for this reason it is important to have some basic understanding of the weather – at least enough to be able to interpret weather forecasts.

Getting Information

Many weather forecasts – on the TV, radio, and in the newspapers – are designed for people on land, and provide limited information for sailing. You will learn a lot more from shipping and inshore water forecasts which will give you the visibility, wind strength in knots, and the likely weather pattern.

Even better, telephone a local Weather Centre. The major ones are manned 24 hours a day, and the forecaster will normally be quite happy to chat to you about your windsurfing prospects.

Wind

Wind is created by differences in atmospheric pressure; and the effect of the land and sea being heated up by the sun.

Highs and lows

When atmospheric pressure is high (called a *high* or anticyclone) the weather is settled and the wind tends to be light. When it is low (called a *low* or depression) you can expect strong winds.

Highs tend to stay pretty much where they are, while lows usually move along fast, with the worst weather (for those on land) right under their centre.

However, the amount of wind depends on the pressure difference (pressure is measured in *millibars*, which is why all yachtsmen watch the barometer) between the *high* and the *low*, as the wind always tends to blow from the former to the latter, and not the other way round.

Sun and sea

The direction and strength of the wind is governed by the atmospheric difference between the *high* and *low*, as the *low* draws wind from the *high*. However this effect is tempered by local conditions, and in particular the effect of the sun as it heats up the land and sea each day.

Every morning the sun heats up the air over the land more quickly than the air over the sea. The hot air from the land starts to rise, and this creates a low pressure area which draws the much cooler air from the sea towards it – in this way an early morning onshore breeze is created. Obviously, this steadily increasing onshore wind is perfect for windsurfing.

As the sun begins to go down, the wind starts to drop, and in a stable weather pattern it will continue to get lighter and lighter. As the sun disappears the land will then cool very rapidly, and reverse the pattern of the morning. A new low pressure area over the water (now warmer than the land) draws the cool air from the land, and an offshore wind builds up.

Exceptions and Dangers

Most areas will have their local weather idiosyncracies. Sometimes these will be quite marked, and you should always do a little preliminary weather research before you sail on an unknown stretch of water.

When there are mountainous areas inland, you can expect the wind to funnel down valleys and blow extremely hard at very short notice. The *Mistral*, which blows down the Rhone Valley to the French Mediterranean, is typical of this – one minute, a steady breeze; five minutes later, a full Force 6.

The Mistral comes suddenly and often unexpectedly, blowing down the Rhône Valley into the Mediterranean. It is an offshore wind which frequently catches out sailors on the south coast of France, and can therefore be very dangerous. Telltale signs are a very clear blue sky with long thin cigar shaped clouds low on the horizon. This sailor has a long journey home in a Force 7 wind.

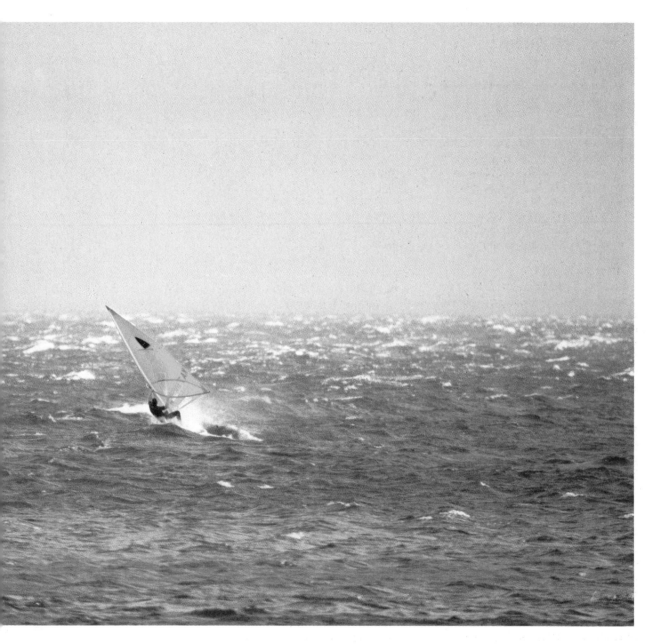

You should also beware when there are mountains or steep hills on the shoreline. With acute differences in temperature on the slopes caused by sunny and shady areas, you may experience sudden and violent downdraughts.

Inland Waters
The sea breeze/land breeze syndrome is primarily of interest to those who sail on the open sea. Apart from the central European and American lakes, few stretches of inland water are large enough for it to have much effect. Their weather pattern is more likely to be changed by the surrounding houses and countryside.

Getting Caught
High temperature and a humid atmosphere cause air to shoot up to a height of around five miles, where it cools very rapidly. The moisture then condenses into rain or hail, and is accompanied by violent gusts and static electricity lightning.

What's happened? It's a thunderstorm, and there will be plenty of warning signs before it happens. When thick cumulus clouds start to soar skywards in a dark tower you know what's coming and you know what to do – get back to the shore or it will catch you on the open sea.

Unpacking the Board

It's an exciting moment when you take delivery of your first board. However, don't get so carried away that you fail to check all the items. All allround and learner boards should have the same elements.

The board itself

Probably wrapped in heavy duty polythene. This may come in handy for storing the board in the winter.

The skeg

This will either slide in; be clipped in with a shockcord to hold it down; or be screwed in – in which case be sure to lubricate the screwholes first. Skegs break and need replacing, and removing corroded screws can be difficult.

The daggerboard

On some you will have to plane down the 'shims'. These are the friction pads that control how tightly the daggerboard fits in its box. Be careful not to overdo this as it will loosen up in the water with use.

The universal joint

This is attached to the *mast foot*, which comes in a variety of shapes and sizes. The top half plugs into the base of the mast, and there should always be some facility for leashing it to the board.

The mast

Either glassfibre or alloy, which may be in two pieces that sleeve together. With some glassfibre masts there is a separate mast tip that is taped into position at the top of the mast.

The wishbone

Rubber covered alloy. There are cleats for the outhaul and inhaul lines, and occasionally you are expected to screw these into position – self-tapping screws will be provided. You will also have an uphaul line.

The sail

If it is bigger than 5.5 sq m, it may

Top: As gear becomes more sophisticated, the number of variations increases. The telescopic wishbone can be lengthened or shortened to suit sails with differing luff perpendicular measurements.

have three glassfibre battens. These are surprisingly easy to lose, so take care of them. Always try and fold the sail along its original creases, and keep it in its bag. Otherwise you can roll it around the mast and stow the whole lot in a mast bag.

Manufacturers' Variations

Some parts are interchangeable between marques – others are not. To change rigs, one simply has to mate the universal joint with the mast foot that fits a particular board. Most wishbones can be used with any rig, but one is normally restricted when it comes to swopping around skegs and daggerboards.

Right: Sailing off into the sunset with a hand painted sail – this one was by Lisa Vincent. If you can't afford a one-off, some sailmakers do screen printing.

Above: There are many different types of mast feet – and they all have different fittings to guarantee exclusivity for their manufacturers.

Assembling the Rig

When it comes to assembling the rig, most systems are very similar. Many new boards are sold with full rigging instructions – if they are not, it should be fairly simple to work out any variations.

You can assemble the rig using the following steps:

1. The sleeve of the sail is slid over the mast, leaving the base of the mast (the broad part) sticking out of the bottom. Most masts are a single length, but some alloy masts are two or three-part extrusions which sleeve together.

2. The universal joint/mast foot is pushed into the base of the mast. This should be an easy fit – take care to remove all sand and grit.

3. The downhaul line is attached between the tack of the sail and the universal joint. One end is tied with a bowline; depending on marque, the other is either lashed, or passes through a cleat.

4. The inhaul line is attached to the mast. This is tied around the mast where there is a gap in the sleeve of the sail. This leaves you about a foot's length to play with – you should tie it so that when the rig is set up the wishbone is approximately at chest height.

The inhaul knot must be pulled very tight so that it does not slip on the mast. On some wishbones there is a slight variation to the knot shown above; both free ends of the line are tied into a single overhand knot, which then fits into a slot in the wishbone.

5. If the sail has battens, these should be slid into their pockets. There are normally retaining lips in the pockets and occasionally there is an elastic strop at its inner end.

6. With the inhaul line, the wishbone is lashed to the mast. It must be attached as rigidly as possible.

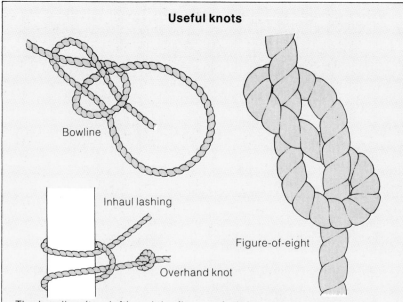

Useful knots

Bowline

Inhaul lashing

Overhand knot

Figure-of-eight

The bowline (top left) and the figure-of-eight are both used in rigging. The inhaul lashing is very simple. On many wishbones, both free ends are tied into the overhand knot, which then slips in to the end of the wishbone.

1 The battens are slid into their pockets and are then held in by a fold of the sailcloth.

2 The uphaul line is attached to the wishbone. It is usually passed through a hole and knotted.

3 Tie knots down the length of the uphaul line to act as hand-holds to pull it up with.

4 The inhaul line must always be firmly attached to the mast at the correct height.

5 When sliding the universal joint into the base of the mast, take care that there is no sand or it will get jammed.

6 The downhaul attaches the clew to the universal joint. It tensions the luff of the sail and governs its shape with the outhaul.

7 The wishbone should be held tightly to the mast – but not so tight that damage is caused when you tighten the outhaul.

8 The outhaul passes from the cleat to the wishbone end; to the clew to the wishbone end; and back to the other cleat.

9 If there is excess line, tie a bowline and leave a large loop. When you grab this, it makes the outhaul easier to adjust.

10 Lay the wishbone parallel to the mast and then pull the outhaul tight. This guarantees a tight lashing at the mast.

7. The long outhaul line is attached and used to draw out the clew.

8. The uphaul line is attached to the wishbone. There should be three or four convenient overhand knots along its length, which will act as handholds. A short piece of shock-cord is tied to the bottom knot – the other end clips to the downhaul line.

9. The downhaul line can now be pulled taut and fastened.

10. Finally, the outhaul line is pulled taut, until the sail is its correct aerofoil shape. Take care not to strain a new sail by pulling it too tight.

Above: 'Flaking' the sail. Take parallel folds while holding the sail on the leech and luff, folding first one way and then the other. Always keep the folds in the same place if possible.

Practice Ashore

Before you take to the water, you can set up the board and the rig on dry land. You can then ensure that everything is correctly set up, and try out the various exercises that you are going to have to do on the water.

You can either place the board flat on the ground with the skeg removed, and then attach the rig to it; or simply stick the mast foot into the ground, without bothering with the board.

You can then try pulling up the rig; walking around it; and sheeting it in and out. By doing this you will get the feel of it before you start, making sure that the wishbone is at the correct height, and that you like the look of the sail.

Setting Up the Rig

It is important that the sail has been set correctly. In moderate conditions of around Force 2 this should require reasonable tension on the downhaul, with the outhaul pulled out within a couple of inches of the end of the wishbone. If there are bad creases, something is very wrong – either with the way you have set the sail (you have most probably overtightened it) or possibly with the sail itself (rather unlikely).

The harder it blows, the flatter the sail should be trimmed, though not absolutely flat, or it will lose all its drive. An overfull sail will be difficult to control in breezy weather, and should be avoided at all costs – it won't even be any good in light winds, when it will fail to harness what little power there is.

The fullness of the sail is determined both by its cut, and the bendiness of the mast. It's unfortunate that many windsurfers are still sold sails that are too full and cheap masts that are too bendy, and that only the very best equipment uses

1 By removing the skeg you can rig the board and practice on dry land before you take to the water.

2 Place the board across the wind, lean back a little and then sheet in to get the feel of the wind.

3 Sheet in a little more and you are 'sailing', leaning back further as the wind increases.

4 Turn the board and try the other tack. (Alternatively you could just bury the mast foot in the sand).

stiff masts and flat sails. A stiff mast is expensive (it needs to be very carefully made of glassfibre, or a tapered alloy extrusion) and a flat sail that still maintains drive is difficult to cut. Hopefully this situation is improving with increasingly refined manufacturing techniques,

as the sails and masts developed by the racing sailors are now rapidly percolating through to the mass market.

Balancing
Carry the board down to the water. The easiest way is with one hand in

the daggerboard case, and the other in the mast foot well.

You can then try standing on it and balancing, with and without the daggerboard. Also try paddling it – when you are inexperienced, it may be the only way to get home.

Carrying the Rig
When you intend to go sailing, leave the board by the water's edge and put the rig in the water first. Left unattended the board would be blown away quite rapidly, whereas the rig is part submerged and drifts very slowly.

The best way to carry the rig is over your head with the luff of the sail facing the direction the wind is coming from. You must always keep it flat and facing in this direction, or the wind is liable to take control and turn you into an involuntary hang-glider.

Fixing the Mast Foot
Take the board into the water alongside the rig, and push the mast foot into its well. It must be a very tight fit which will only come out if there is a lot of pressure – for example if the mast or one of your limbs will break if it doesn't.

Having a mast foot that comes out of its well at inopportune moments is incredibly frustrating, and can be dangerous. Most modern mast feet have a gland that can be tightened or loosened, or alternatively you can wrap the mast foot with insulating tape to pad it out and make it a perfect fit – this was always necessary on the old Windsurfer wooden T-pieces.

Leashing the Mast Foot
The mast foot must be leashed to the hull, so that if it comes out, it is still attached to the board. Most modern boards have a leashing system with a strop or a lanyard, but if it's not provided you must improvise something with a short length of line that can do the job equally well.

Carrying the Board
You should carry the rig over your head, with the wishbone pointing directly into the direction the wind is coming from. Keep it level, and don't let the wind get under or on top of it.

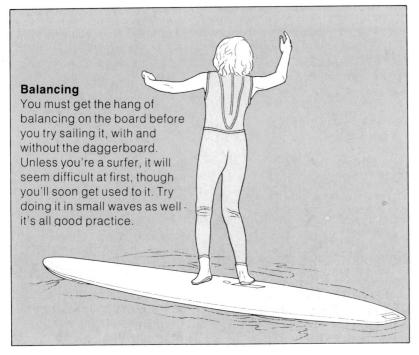

Balancing
You must get the hang of balancing on the board before you try sailing it, with and without the daggerboard. Unless you're a surfer, it will seem difficult at first, though you'll soon get used to it. Try doing it in small waves as well - it's all good practice.

Getting Under Way

When you get started, the board should be in deep enough water for you to put in the whole length of the daggerboard – standing by the board, the water need not come up any higher than your thighs.

Before you hop on the board it's best to line it up so that everything is set for getting under way; you want the wind blowing on to your back with the rig lying away from you.

At first, just hold the uphaul line with one hand, and try and get comfortably balanced before you attempt to pull up the rig.

Find out the most comfortable position for your feet as well as your body. On most boards they should be close together on the centreline of the board, just between the mast foot and the daggerboard case. On some boards you can put a foot forward of the mast, which will help to keep the rig inclined forwards; others won't have enough buoyancy in the bow, and you will have to keep your weight back to avoid submarining when under way.

When you pull up the rig, you will be amazed by how heavy it seems. The sail and the mast sleeve are full of water, and with the wind holding the sail down it seems like a ton weight until it's clear of the water. Getting over this is simply a matter of technique, but for a beginner it always makes it important to have an undersized sail.

Once you've got the clew clear of the water, rest and get comfortably balanced once again. You can then stop and work out where the wind is coming from. Then incline the rig fore and aft, which will turn the board in the direction your require.

Pulling up the rig. Place your feet close together on the centreline of the board. It's normally easiest if one is just aft of the mast while the other is in front of it. Then take the uphaul line.

Pull the rig up hand over hand until the clew is clear of the water. It will seem very heavy. The sleeve is full of water which drains away once it is upright, and while the clew drags, the wind will hold it down against the water. Therefore it's less tiring to pull it up quickly.

Make sure the wind is behind you and pull the rig a little way out of the water. If it is not on the beam, the board and rig will now slew around until it is. Lean back against the weight of the rig.

Getting going. Take a re____ ___
balance, with both hands holding
the uphaul line near the wishbone.
Keep the wind blowing across the
board – if you incline the rig
forward it will bear away, while if
you incline it aft it will head up.
When you're ready, reach out with
your forward hand and grab the
wishbone a little way back from the
mast. You can then let go the
uphaul line with your other hand,
and get the hang of holding the rig
just like that, before you try sailing.
Like most points of learning it will
seem very wobbly when you start
but will get easier all the time.

When you feel confident, incline
the rig a little way into the wind, and
reach out with your after hand
which will become your sheet
hand. Grab the wishbone a couple
of feet back from your mast hand –
the CE should be somewhere
roughly between them, and you
want to control it as well as
possible. You can then lean back a
little, and gradually sheet in with
the after hand until the sail stops
flapping. You must keep the rig
inclined into the direction the wind
is coming from all the time – ie
raked forward. If you don't, the
board will immediately begin to
head up into the wind.

Once you sheet in, the board will
start moving. So long as you're in
balance it will go straight.

When you want to stop, let go with
the sheet hand. If you're in a hurry,
let go of everything.

That will bring you to a dead halt
very quickly. You can then get
going again.

Sailing a Course

When you try getting under way, the wind must be on the beam, blowing across the board at right angles. There is no need to hurry, for the procedure can be followed step-by-step, with pauses in between the stages. All the time you must rest and get the feel of what you're doing until you feel comfortable: holding the rig with the uphaul line; holding the wishbone with your mast hand; and holding the wishbone with both hands.

Once you start sailing a course, you will find out the best way of holding the wishbone. In moderate winds you will want the mast hand to be around six inches behind the mast, with the boom hand another 18 inches or so further back. The CE will be centred right in the middle, between your hands, and if you feel uncomfortable and unbalanced you must move your hands

Remember that once you are sailing, you have to observe the Rules of the Road, whether or not you are in control of the board.

In this instance, starboard (the dinghy) has right of way over port (the windsurfer). This should be tempered with common sense.

Bearing away

To bear away, the sailor needs to rake the rig forward, while gradually sheeting out the sail as the wind goes further behind. When the wind is directly behind (running) you sail with the rig at right angles to it.

You need to keep your balance throughout the manoeuvre. Foot position is important, and you must move your weight inboard as the sideways pull on the sail slackens. It helps to give some sharp pulls with the sheet hand to help the board bear away. You will also find that you can help a conventional board bear away if you push down the windward side.

Heading up

To head up, you rake the rig aft, sheeting in until you are on a beat. In light winds you will then have the wishbone close to your body with your arms bent.

The beat is a difficult point of sailing for the learner. You must sail as close as possible to the wind, without going so close that the wind begins to strike the sail on the leeward side and the board rounds up so that it is facing directly into the wind.

In light winds, sail with the rig raked a little forward; your arms bent; and the sail just starting to flutter a very little.

until you find the correct position. As it blows harder you will need to shift your grip as the CE moves further aft, and you can experiment by grasping the boom with an over and underhand grip – whichever feels better.

Altering Course

You can alter course on a board as easily and rapidly as with the rudder on a boat. Weather conditions make a difference. If it's blowing hard with big waves and you're sailing a sensitive board with a rounded hull, it will react instantaneously.

Altering course works basically on the principle of CE over CLR. If you want to head up into the wind you rake the rig aft; if you want to bear away from the wind you rake it forward. Once you are on the desired new course, get the rig back into its original position, which will be inclined slightly forward, and trim the sail accordingly. Next, practise sailing a wavy course – heading up and bearing away.

The Points of Sailing

1. Running. Travelling in the same direction as the wind.

There is no suction on the sail and the effect of the wind is ameliorated. To steer, you must bank the sail to either side.

2. Reaching. The wind on or nearly on the beam, and less pressure on the daggerboard makes this the fastest and easiest point of sailing. If the wind is coming from behind it is a broad reach; if it is coming from ahead it is a close reach.

3. Beating. Sailing as close to the wind as possible in order to claw up to windward. Depending on your skill and your board, you can normally sail within 30 degrees of the direction the wind is coming from.

Tacking

In order to sail towards the direction the wind is coming from, you need to sail a zig-zag course. This is called tacking.

As you try to reach the point you wish to get to, you sail on one tack and then on the other (port and starboard) as it suits you. Governing factors on the tacks you choose are liable to be the prevailing conditions, obstructions en route, or simply tacking for the sake of a change.

Your port and starboard tacks should be contained within a maximum arc of around 90 degrees – any more, and you will sail a very long way to get to where you want.

As you get more experienced, the arc between your tacks should come down to around 60 degrees, depending on how close to the wind the board you sail will point. This is governed by the board itself – the efficiency of its rig, its shape, and its daggerboard, allied to weather conditions – as well as your skill. You must sail the board close to the wind, but not too close or it will lose power and stall as the wind comes increasingly on the leeward side of the sail.

Judging just how close to sail is largely a matter of experience and technique, but a board will always head up into the wind when inexperienced hands are not keeping the rig raked far enough forwards. The telltale sign is when the sail begins to lift – the wind on the leeward side will start pushing the area around the window in the sail towards you. Unless you react and bear away, the board will continue to round up and eventually deposit you in the water.

When you change tacks, your

There are many ways of tacking, and as you get more experienced your technique will get more refined and change a little to suit every occasion.

For a basic easy tack you head up by raking the rig aft (**1**). Continue raking if aft until the clew is over the centreline of the board (**2**) which will soon be facing directly into the wind (**3**). At this point transfer your sheet hand to the uphaul line, a few inches from the wishbone. Then start to move round the front of the mast, transferring your mast hand to the uphaul as you do so, and continuing to rake the rig aft. Move round the other side of the board, while the clew swings over the stern and into the wind.

movements should be smooth and unfussy. The object is to get the board sailing on the opposite tack, and you don't need to stick rigidly to a set of rules in order to do so.

All you want to do is to turn the board through the eye of the wind, and then start off again on your new tack. At first you can simply swing the rig round the stern, taking little steps with your feet so that the board swings round as well. You then get into position for the new tack with the wind behind you and the rig to leeward, and get under way once again.

As self confidence and skill increase, you can speed up this manoeuvre, turning the board by inclining the rig aft, and moving round the *front* of the mast. As the nose of the board passes through the eye of the wind, you catch the wishbone on the new side, rake the rig forward, sheet in, and head off on the new tack, taking it easy all the time. You will find you get faster and your technique gets better.

Next rake the rig forward, and transfer your new mast hand to the wishbone. Grab it with your new sheet hand, and then sheet in and sail off on the new tack. For a far faster tack, as the clew swings over the centreline, the sailor grabs the mast with his mast hand (**4**). He then transfers his sheet hand to the mast as he moves round the front of it (**5**). Next he throws the rig forward into the new tack, while reaching out to sheet in with his new sheet hand (**6**). As he does so, he rapidly moves his other hand from the mast to the wishbone (**7**) and continues sheeting in (**8**).

Gybing

Gybing is the opposite of tacking. Rather than the nose of the board passing through the eye of the wind, it is the stern that passes through it, with the wind behind the board. Like tacking, gybing is a matter of technique – but there are even more variations. In. its simplest form – the rope gybe – it is one of the easiest manoeuvres to execute.

Power Gybe

The basic gybe is the rope gybe. You sail on a dead run, and then incline the rig well to windward so that the board bears away. As the stern passes through the eye of the wind, transfer your hands to the uphaul line (sheet hand before mast hand). Let the rig swing round and then grab the wishbone on the new side with your new mast hand and sheet hand.

The power gybe illustrated will speed up the process of turning so that the board changes direction a great deal more quickly and dramatically.

1 Let go the wishbone with your mast hand and grab the mast.

2 Give the wishbone a shove with your sheet hand.

3 Let go the wishbone as the rig swings round, and transfer that hand to the mast.

4 Grab the wishbone with your new sheet hand.

5 Sheet in hard to spin the board round. This will be quicker if you sink the stern of the board.

6 Take up sailing on the new tack.

Flare Gybe

The flare gybe looks very neat.
1 Start off on a run.
2 Begin to incline the rig well to windward.
3 If it's windy you may be travelling fast, so you need to slow the board down. To do so, step back so that the stern begins to drag in the water.
4 You can also steer the board through the gybe by pushing down the windward side. On a roundboard this will make the board turn much faster.
5 Carry on turning the board so that the stern passes through the eye of the wind and you have turned so far that the clew of the sail is facing into the direction the wind is coming from.
6 Transfer your mast hand to the sail, and let go with your sheet hand. The rig will whip round to a broad-reaching position, so that you can reach out with your new sheet hand and sail away without losing speed throughout the entire manoeuvre.

The power gybe and the flare gybe get more and more rarefied as the wind increases and techniques improve to match it. Hawaiian sailors are the world leaders in high speed gybing on short boards. With a lot of practice they can gybe in a very short space at full speed — an art which the regatta sailor also has to master.

Safety

Windsurfing can be dangerous unless you follow basic rules which make it safe – otherwise you'll risk drowning yourself and giving the sport a bad name. Here are the most important rules:

1. Don't go off sailing in a strong offshore wind unless there is assistance to hand. Unless you have requested help (should you need it) before setting off, you should never need to be rescued. Don't be the cause of a major air-sea rescue search – it costs the taxpayer a lot of money and it wastes a lot of time.

2. Check out the weather forecast carefully before you leave. If strong winds are forecast, take heed, and act accordingly.

3. Check out tides and other dangers. If you're in a warm country, you don't want to step on a sea urchin. Worse still, you don't want a shark to mistake the bottom of your board for some nice soft white underbelly.

4. Be very careful of the cold. It catches up on you faster than you think, so dress up, not down. In most circumstances you should wear a wetsuit and footwear as a matter of course. If it's really cold, you can wear a dry suit, but be very careful. You can't swim well in it, and if you lose your board you'll just have to bob up and down like the Michelin man.

5. Can you swim? You shouldn't be going windsurfing in the first place if you can't. If you have any doubts about your ability to cope with the conditions, wear a buoyancy aid.

6. Check every detail of your board. Is anything likely to break? You'll be really stuck if the mast foot gives out. Carry a towline which you can also use as a replacement if the outhaul or inhaul lines break – the neatest way is to carry it wound tightly around the after end of the wishbone.

If you're going to use a harness, always carry spare harness lines as well.

You must leash the mast foot to the board. If you have a bad fall, and the board, the rig, and you part company, you'll have a major problem getting it all back together again.

7. Learn the right of way rules. You need to know who has right of way, but don't push your luck. The other sailor might not be so well clued up, and you should make every effort to avoid a collision even if you are in the right.

8. Keep out of the way of shipping. Narrow channels and shipping should be avoided at all costs. Ships can't stop or alter course – if you mess them about you deserve to be banned from the water.

9. Avoid swimmers. They have as much right to the water as you do, and they aren't so manoeuvrable. A board can accelerate to ten or 15 knots pretty easily, and that's quite fast enough to kill your first swimmer!

10. Never abandon your board. It will continue floating long after you can, and it can be paddled for longer than you can swim.

11. Learn the International Distress Signals. Then at least someone will know you're drowning and not just waving.

12. Don't go out at night or in the fog. It's a very good way to get lost – two Swedish windsurfers went one better and got lost for good that way. Remember also that sharks come out for dinner when it's dark.

13. If you go out alone, tell someone what you're up to. It's OK to go out alone if you're sure you can handle it, but tell someone what you're up to just in case things go wrong.

14. Learn self-help techniques before you need them. You should find out just how easy it is to stow the rig and paddle the board. Different boards have different requirements – you should also find out what it's like being towed behind a motor boat.

15. Recognize hypothermia. Hypothermia is the condition when you start to get cold (just shivering) and then carry on getting colder. The final stages are unconsciousness followed by drowning, and in northern waters it doesn't take long to get to them.

Not only do you get cold when you're hypothermic, but you also get weak and apathetic. The process becomes a vicious circle of falling off your board and getting colder and weaker, so that you fall off the board again and again and again. . . .

For a windsurfer, the answer is to come ashore as soon as you start to feel cold and tired. If you can, have a hot shower, and get into some warm clothes as soon as possible.

If you decide to stay out on the water, then you're looking for trouble. If you're stuck out there and can't get back, then you're in trouble.

If you're on the board, you must try and keep the blood circulation going while you're battling against the *chill factor* induced by the wind – you've got to keep warm and paddle the board towards help.

If you're in the water, don't leave the board and swim unless it's clearly the best answer. Water conducts heat away from the body 26 times faster than still air, and if you can keep your head above the water, you should go into the HELP huddle, with your legs tightly crossed and your arms wrapped round your body.

16. Choose the right sail area. There's no point in going out if you can't handle the conditions with the rig you've got. A board with a small rig that is in control will go much faster than one with a bigger rig that is out of control – and it will get you home as well.

This is Baron Arnaud de Rosnay attempting to windsurf the English Channel for a wager, and being rescued for his pains. He left his board behind, and no one knows who claimed it.

Self-Help

In some circumstances you will have to pack up the rig and paddle home – either if something breaks, or if you're inexperienced and can't handle the conditions.

Sit down on the board facing the direction the wind is coming from; then take out the mast foot and undo the leash. Push the rig away from the mast first, so that the board blows downwind away from it. You can then undo the outhaul, and, starting at the clew, roll the sail up tightly until you get to the mast. Then lash the end of the wishbone near the top of the mast with the outhaul line, wrapping it around as much of the sail as possible at the same time. You should do the same with the uphaul at the lower end of the mast.

You can then put the stowed rig on the board, lashing it if possible so that it doesn't get dislodged by the waves.

Wind

Top: With the board blowing downwind away from the rig, you can undo the outhaul and roll the sail from the clew. It should be a tight roll at the mast, which can then be lashed with the uphaul line and outhaul line, with the wishbone tied alongside.

Above: You can then put the whole rig on the board, with the mast foot facing forward. If you can, lash it so it won't slide off the board when you are paddling. If you are in real trouble, don't have any compunction about leaving the rig behind if you need to.

The best way to paddle is by lying on the board (above left). Alternatively you can kneel or sit astride it. If you can find someone to give you a tow, you can grab hold of his mast foot and lie alongside (above right), keeping the boards as close together as possible.

You will find both techniques surprisingly difficult. It is best to find out just how difficult before you need to use them in earnest, when there won't be time for any mistakes – it's a long hard struggle getting back upwind like this when it's blowing hard.

The international distress signal (left) is to wave your arms slowly back and forth over your head. You must use it so people appreciate you are not just waving.

Top: It is possible to buy a very expensive harness that contains a proper lifejacket. This will float you face up while unconscious. It can be inflated orally, or by a CO₂ cylinder activated by a ripcord, and is not in the least bulky to wear when uninflated.

Above: Harnesses are dealt with in detail on pages 92–93. They are a potential source of danger, particularly if the hook gets entangled with the harness line. For this reason you must always have a quick-release system on the harness, and better still on the hook. You can then use it with complete safety.

Paddling

You can either lie or kneel on the board, paddling it with your hands. It is generally easier with the dag-gerboard retracted or removed. If things look really grim, you should have no compunction about abandoning the rig, which will be great-ly hindering your progress. If you have been sensible, it will have been insured, so it can be replaced.

You'll need to be careful not to get broadside on to waves, which will roll over both board and rig.

Flares

If you're sailing alone in rough water, carrying flares is a sensible precaution. You can get small packs of flares specially designed for windsurfing. You can carry them strapped to your leg, or in a harness pack, or in a sail pocket.

Lifejackets

A lifejacket supports the head above water – a buoyancy aid does not.

Most lifejackets are far too bulky for windsurfing, but in some cases it may be worth sailing with a CO_2/ orally inflated lifejacket that can be combined with a harness and won't constrict movement or get in the way.

Reefing

If the wind blows up and catches you out, it would be ideal to be able to reef the sail as you can on a yacht. Sailmakers have tried out various ideas with zips etc, but unfortunately none have worked very well.

There are two ways of reefing a conventional windsurfing sail. Either you can take it off the mast and re-rig it without the bottom panels beneath the wishbone – somehow you'll have to roll them up into a neat bundle. Alternative-ly, a better method is to undo the outhaul, slacken the downhaul, and attempt to roll the top half of the sail around the mast. It will stay rolled when you make up the out-haul, and even though the shape will look pretty odd, you'll lose around one-third of the sail's area. It's sensible to try this method out before you need to resort to it in earnest, as its degree of success will vary depending on the rig.

Handling Stronger Winds

When the wind is light and the sea is flat, most people can master windsurfing in a few days. As long as you have enough balancing ability to ride a bicycle, and understand what the rig is doing, there should be no problems.

However, this type of windsurfing is fine in hot weather if you've nothing better to do. Otherwise it can be a little boring, particularly when you see the speeds at which other windsurfers travel when it blows hard. As the lift from their sails is combined with a light board/body weight, they are planing while you are displacement sailing. This means that your board is sailing through the water and its speed is governed by its length, while theirs is skimming over the water having broken through the displacement barrier.

When a board starts to plane, the proportional increase in speed is enormous, and so is the fun. To counter the force of the wind you must lean back with your body close to the water, while the board hisses and dances beneath your feet, with a shower of spray on each side. When you've done it once, you're hooked.

The Problems

Because it displaces so little wetted area, an Open Class roundboard will start to plane very easily – in Force 2 with a skilled sailor. The flat board is pushing more water, and consequently takes more wind to break free and plane – say Force 3 or 4.

This is the wind speed barrier that you need to surmount, and you will find it more difficult than mastering the initial stages of windsurfing. It is the barrier where many people give up.

1. The wind
When the wind is less than Force 2, there is little pull in the sail. You can control the rig as you want it.

As the wind speed increases the rig will pull harder, and when it

Above: Jumping demands a high level of fitness, combined with first-class technique.

starts getting on for Force 4, the problems will start.

Everything happens so much quicker. You can't pull the rig up out of the water, as the wind pressure is holding it down, and with several gallons of water trapped in the sail and its sleeve, you seem to be pulling up an immense weight. Your strength is sapped, and when you get it up, you find you cannot counter the force of the wind – the rig is blown from your hands by a gust, or worse still you hang on and it takes you with it.

2. The waves
When there is wind, there are likely to be waves. If you're sailing in a strong wind on the sea and there aren't any waves, it means that you are sailing off a weather shore and are very likely to get blown out to sea. The onshore wind is safe, but with surf breaking on the shoreline and the board being thrown everywhere, how do you stay on your feet?

Inshore waters won't have such big waves. The smaller and less exposed the area, the smaller you

will find the waves – but then you'll be plagued by a gusty wind caused by the obstructions on shore.

Either way you have the problem of controlling increased pressure in the sail, with a very unstable board beneath your feet, a fitful and gusty wind, or both.

3. Strength
The reason many people give up windsurfing at this stage is that they believe they are not strong enough.

Lifting the rig, controlling it, falling off the board and attempting to get going again, all seem to sap an inordinate amount of energy – particularly when sailing in a cold climate.

The Answers

Through lack of knowledge you make it harder for yourself. Strong winds are handled by *technique* and *equipment*, and though strength is important, Force 4 sailing can be enjoyed by anyone of average physical fitness. As the wind increases, so must your technique improve – only extreme conditions will demand unusual strength.

There are three main rules for strong wind sailing. Once you master them, you master your board:

1. Understand the theory
You must know why the board and rig are behaving the way they are.
2. Master the technique
You cannot hope to fight wind and waves on equal terms. You must learn when and how to give in to them, so that they can be exploited to best advantage.
3. Use the right equipment
'I can't lift the rig' may mean lack of strength or technique, but it may simply be solved by putting on a smaller sail. The harsher the conditions, the easier the board must be to sail.

Right: Getting started in strong winds is particularly difficult, and it doesn't help if there is surf breaking under your board.

Suitable Boards

Generally speaking, the most suitable board for strong winds is one that is flat and stable. Roundboards may be faster over a wider range of conditions, but when the going gets rough they are considerably more difficult to sail, and only of interest for triangle racing.

Once a flatboard is planing, it is going fast. For use in strong winds it should have enough buoyancy, particularly in the bow, to support the sailor, with adequate rocker to carry it through waves.

The board should be strong enough to cope with the considerable stresses of sailing through waves, and even stronger to survive the battering it will get when the waves sweep you on to the beach.

Below: This strong wind board can be controlled with the footstraps, straightened, and landed flat.

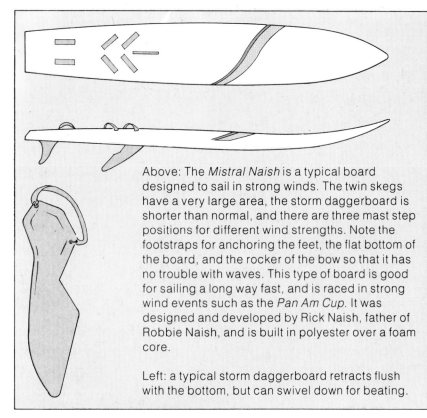

Above: The *Mistral Naish* is a typical board designed to sail in strong winds. The twin skegs have a very large area, the storm daggerboard is shorter than normal, and there are three mast step positions for different wind strengths. Note the footstraps for anchoring the feet, the flat bottom of the board, and the rocker of the bow so that it has no trouble with waves. This type of board is good for sailing a long way fast, and is raced in strong wind events such as the *Pan Am Cup*. It was designed and developed by Rick Naish, father of Robbie Naish, and is built in polyester over a foam core.

Left: a typical storm daggerboard retracts flush with the bottom, but can swivel down for beating.

Another famous design developed from the Hawaiian *Pan Am Cup* (above and left). The *Marker M1* is designed by the top German strong wind sailor, Jürgen Honsheid, and has more buoyancy than the Naish board opposite. The unusual daggerboard swivels vertically for beating, and then retracts into the hull for offwind work, so that only the tip is exposed.

Right: The most extreme extension of a strong wind board is a very light (say 12 kg), short (say 270 cm) projectile, with a single skeg at the back. Very difficult to sail, a board such as this can only be used in Force 4 +.

As the wind increases, the CE needs to be moved further from the CLR to prevent the board from rounding up into the wind owing to increased pressure in the sail. There are several ways of tackling this problem. The mast step can be moved forward, and/or the dagger-board moved aft. The daggerboard area can be greatly diminished while the size of the skegs is increased.

Generally, the sailor will need to stand further back on the board, keeping the bow clear of the waves. The board must have an excellent non-slip finish, and when you have got the hang of them, footstraps anchor your feet in position and make it a great deal easier to stay in control.

Right: A flat, buoyant board such as the *Windsurfer* always responds well to a strong wind, and is more fun with a storm daggerboard.

Rigs and Sails

Just as a yacht reefs its sails as the wind blows harder, so a windsurfer must change to a more manageable size of sail.

From this point of view windsurfing is not a cheap sport. The strong wind enthusiast will need three or more sails specifically for the job. As a rough guide, the size of sail you use depends on your ability and weight (a big sailor carries a bigger sail), as well as on the conditions.

So, for medium to strong wind use (Force 4) you will need a sail of around 5.8 sq m, dropping to 5.2 sq m as the wind increases. For Force 6 and more 4.1 sq m would be about right, and for children or in really difficult conditions you could drop down to 3 sq m.

Unless you are triangle racing, a fibreglass mast is preferable. It is more resilient than alloy, and if it breaks in the surf it can often be repaired. It is a good idea to reinforce the boom slot area with fibreglass tape. For sails of 5 sq m and above you can use a regular length wishbone, but with smaller sails it is an advantage to have a short LP for a shorter wishbone of

An IYRU *Open Class* regatta sail. It can be used by experts up to around Force 5, but at 6.3 sq m would overpower most sailors.

A smaller sail within the Open Class rules. It can be more easily handled in a blow, and has a high clew to ride over waves.

A straight leech strong wind sail of around 6 sq m. Any bigger and it would need a battened roach.

The Fathead, with a short LP and wide head, supported by two full length battens.

As the strong wind sails get smaller, they develop a hollow leech which brings the CE forward. Note the large windows.

Smaller still, say 4.8 sq m, and this sail has a shorter LP for a short wishbone which makes for easier handling, but puts up the cost.

Smallest of all, say 4 sq m or less, this sail is shorter in the luff so that it's very easy to control with the CE low down.

Left: A typical strong wind sail, of around 5.5 sq m. Note the hollow leech with no battens. With the mast foot well forward to prevent luffing, the rig must be raked right back on the beats, so the clew has to be cut very high.

Below: A Fathead is used in waves, the theory being that the large area of sail at the top of the mast picks up the wind while the board is in the troughs. However it is more prone to damage. The board is a swallowtail design sailed by Malte Simmer off the Hawaiian island of Maui. It is a typical very light, short board.

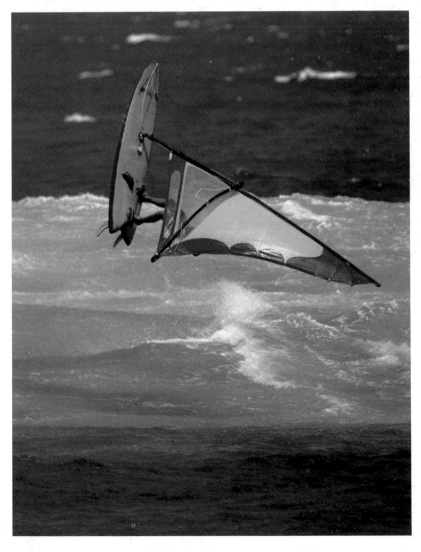

around 2.1 m. This will be much easier to handle – less leverage and less to pull out of the water.

Remember that the clew should always be pulled out to the end of the wishbone. It should also be cut high, so that when the mast foot is well forward, the rig can be raked well aft, without dragging in the water.

Construction and Design

Strong wind sails should take a lot of hard wear. The cloth weight should be at least 3.8 oz, getting heavier as the size of the sail diminishes.

Battens should be avoided. If the sail is bigger than 6 sq m it will need them to support a roach, but otherwise they are an unnecessary complication and an added expense. They are also liable to break and damage the sail.

The exception is the 'Fathead' sail, which has a short LP to get the benefits of a short wishbone, together with a square-shaped head that is held out by a couple of battens. The theory is that the added area at the top gives more power in the troughs of waves, but it seems more likely that conventional straight or hollow leech sails are cheaper to buy, easier to look after and just as efficient.

Getting Going

The board should be very carefully prepared for sailing in stronger winds.

The mast step should be firmly in place, if necessary jammed in with black plastic sticky tape. Most important of all – THE RIG MUST BE LEASHED TO THE HULL. If you wipe out, and the rig, board, and yourself become separated – you have problems. First you have to swim for the board, and if it's a light one it may be blown downwind faster than you can catch it. Then (hopefully) you have to paddle for the rig, which may have sunk in the meantime.

Make sure *all lashings on the rig are correctly done*: the outhaul, downhaul, and wishbone lashing. If the *non-slip·finish is not good enough* (all over the board), apply some

The beach start is the neatest form of launching, but can only work if there is a cross wind, and the board with its daggerboard does not draw more than 45 cm. **(1)** Holding the board with one hand at the stern, and the mast with the other, the board is slid into the sea **(2)** until there is enough water for it to float free. The sailor hops on, stretching out with his sheet hand **(3)**, and then sheets in and sails away **(4)**. It takes practice and confidence to get it right.

board wax, which you should be able to buy from a windsurf shop.

Check the skeg – make sure it won't pop out or fall off. If there is any chance of *losing the daggerboard*, lash that as well.

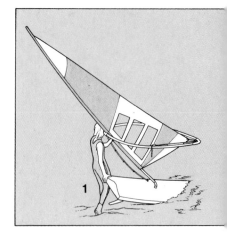

Below: Two different ways of launching. The Windsurfer in the foreground is trying a beach start while the sailor behind him is pulling his board out through the surf, looking for flat water.

Be sure to carry a good *length of spare line*. You can use it as a towrope, and if anything breaks (harness lines do so constantly) it's useful in reserve.

Conditions

Are they suitable? If there is an offshore wind, are you going to be able to get back? Are there any strong currents? How cold is the water? What's the weather forecast?

Windsurfers often ignore these questions, and then find that they can't beat back through a gusty offshore wind that's increasing all the time. They fall into cold water with increasing regularity, as they become progressively less capable of handling the board. Then the tide turns and begins to sweep them down the coast – with luck they get rescued and simply cause a lot of trouble to everyone else, but a few get drowned.

With forethought and common-sense all will be well:

1. Check that conditions are suitable.
2. Check the weather.
3. Don't use a sail that's too big.
4. Wear the right clothing.
5. Check the board thoroughly.
6. Let someone know what you're up to before you leave.

Getting on the Water

If the water is relatively flat, you can launch in the normal way.

If there is any surf, you must pull your board out through the breaking water, and hopefully find

Below: The water start is another way of getting going. With your feet on the side of the board, you wait for the wind in the rig to lift you out of the water and get sailing. Not easy!

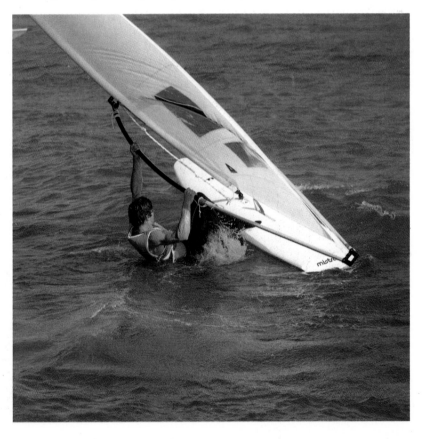

a flat spot between the waves where you can hop on quickly and get going. If the wind is blowing across your launch place, you can go for the nifty 'beach start', which looks good to spectators, and is not as difficult as you would imagine. The sequence is on the previous page, and the main point to remember is to keep the board beam on to the wind, and not let it round up.

Getting Under Way

Getting under way in strong winds gets progressively more difficult as the wind speed increases.

If there are any waves, you've got a problem staying on the board, let alone sailing it – but even on flat water it's tricky.

Think out the problems first. There is much more force in the sail, and therefore a more powerful CE. This means that whereas the board would sail in a straight line in lighter winds, the CE is now pushing harder so that the board is constantly rounding up into the wind.

You can solve this problem by technique or equipment – it will probably be a combination of both:

1. Equipment

On pages 78–79 we looked at suitable strong wind boards, which have big skegs, small daggerboards, and their mast feet further from the daggerboard case than the norm – in other words with the CE moved further from the CLR.

On pages 80–81 we looked at rigs and sails, where the trend is to have a shorter LP and hollow leeches, both of which will help to move the CE forward.

Boards and rigs specifically designed for strong wind use will have some or all of these features in various combinations, while allround boards can be adapted with minor changes of detail – for instance with a storm daggerboard and hollow leech sail, the Windsurfer becomes an easy board to sail in strong winds.

Sailing a flatboard upwind, the sailor keeps his feet near the edge when it's blowing hard.

2. Technique

When sailing in stronger winds you hang beneath the rig, so that it supports your weight. The reasons for this are:

1. The more a yacht heels, the less heeling effect the wind has on its

On a roundboard (above and below) the feet are kept on the edge to control the amount of 'rail' – how much the board is allowed to heel due to pressure from the mast foot and daggerboard. Getting it up to the right angle without flipping it right over is an art which only a few excel in. It enables them to 'powersail' upwind at tremendous speeds.

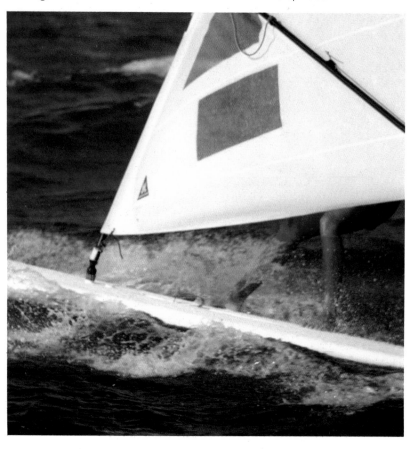

sails – to be able to cope with the strength of the wind, you must heel your rig on a windsurfer.

2. The rig lifts the board. In effect it makes it lighter, so that it planes more easily and goes faster.

Getting Under Way by Numbers

Getting the rig up out of the water is your first problem. The wind catches it when it is still very full of water, so with the mast tip a few inches clear of the surface, you must wait until the board slews round into the wind, which will get under the rig, and help lift it for you. You can then rapidly haul it clear, back it to get to the wind abeam position, and stand by to take off.

If it's rough, you've got to get going straight away – if the water is flat you can take your time.

Bearing in mind the problems with your CE, you must be prepared to grasp the wishbone considerably further back than you have been used to – you can then rake the mast to windward until it touches your shoulder. The sheet hand then sheets in gradually, while you let your weight fall back to be supported by the sail. If the board begins to luff, cant the rig sharply to windward, sheet in, and if necessary push the front of the board away with your foot.

Once you can prevent the board from luffing, you have mastered the art of getting under way in strong winds.

Sailing Upwind

Beating has similar problems to 'getting under way' – for example, the board always wants to luff. Even boards that are specifically set up for strong winds can have this problem, as most of them are designed primarily for reaching.

The trick is to always keep the rig raked forward, and counter the gusts by raking it further forward still, while playing the sheet hand to feather the sail.

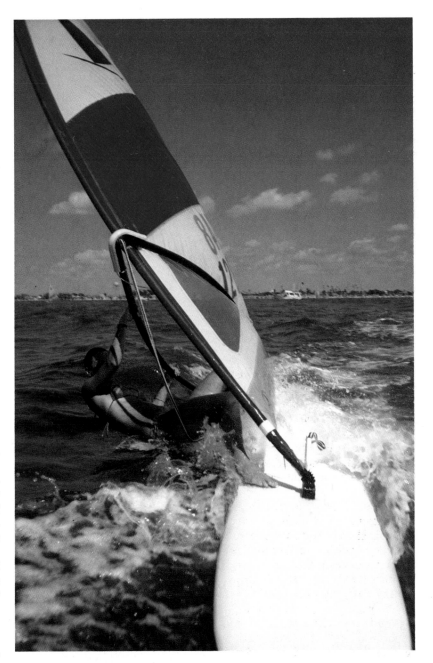

To point high, you need a full daggerboard, but you can sail fast and free with a storm daggerboard (or if it's very windy, skegs alone) without the problems of railing or luffing.

Be wary of lulls. When the wind drops suddenly, the trick is to do a knees bend and bring your weight inboard rapidly.

In strong winds you can pull the daggerboard a little to help prevent the board from luffing. Note that the clew is sheeted right into the centreline of the board, and the sailor's feet are right on the edge and close together for upwind sailing. In a lull, she will have to swing her body weight inboard immediately.

Falls

Getting going in stronger winds is difficult enough, but once under way, and even in relatively flat water, one's first impression may be that the board is behaving in a temperamental manner.

Catapult Falls

Once you have got started in stronger winds, the catapult fall is liable to be your first major problem. Sailing along happily on a reach, or bearing away, a gust hits the rig and the sailor strains to keep his balance and hold the wishbone. However the wind is too strong. He is plucked off his feet and vaulted into the rig, rather like going over the handlebars of a bicycle.

Of course. this can be fun for shore watchers, but it soon gets tiring, and if you are catapulted into the mast or the front of the board it can be expensive and dangerous. A head is quite capable of breaking a mast and the surface of the board is quite capable of breaking a head.

There are two alternatives:

1. Leave it!

It doesn't take long to know when you can't handle it. Another second and you will be lifted off your feet, so LET GO! In a light wind, letting go with the boom hand would have sufficed, but in this case let go with both hands – and abort gracefully backwards into the water. Nothing will be damaged, and you will have used considerably less strength than being swung through the air, and then having to retrieve the board and pick up the pieces.

2. Handle it!

As your technique improves, so should your need to 'Leave it!' diminish.

Like getting under way, success in averting a catapult fall depends on your ability to understand and handle the rig. When the gust comes, the sail must be feathered into the wind. The mast hand banks the rig to windward while the boom hand lets out the sail, spilling out the wind. It's a knack which you soon pick up, reacting in time with the wind.

Sometimes conditions are so unpredictable that you need more

On a flat board this will only tend to happen on reaches, when the board is going really fast. On a roundboard, due to its speed and a shape which encourages it to roll over, it will happen upwind as well.

There are two ways to deal with this problem:

1. Weight

As the board tips, shift your feet to the windward rail to push it down. Once back to normal, shift your weight inboard again.

On a roundboard with the mast foot pushing, you need to do this all the time. You may rake the daggerboard aft a little, but if you are racing you will need most of it down.

Therefore a very different technique – 'railing' – becomes necessary. These racing boards benefit from being sailed slightly on edge, since it increases their efficiency upwind. On this point, a roundboard is positively encouraged to sail on its side, while the sailor controls the amount of 'rail' with his feet on the windward edge, pushing down as the rail rides up too much, and letting it rise up if it's too far down. All the time he's doing knee bends to achieve this, with his torso held rigid by the harness line, sheeting the sail in and out as necessary.

However, most strong wind sailing is done on flatboards, and with these, capsize falls can be counteracted by:

2. The daggerboard

It is the daggerboard that is the main problem on a flatboard. Withdraw it, or cut down its area, and the problem is removed.

Therefore, if you are sailing for fun, replace your daggerboard with a storm daggerboard of only one-third of its depth – not enough to aquaplane on.

Alternatively, if you have a daggerboard that retracts into the hull, you can sail with just a few inches beneath the board.

Your third option is to 'pull' it, see overleaf.

Above and left: The catapult fall at its most dramatic. The sailor doesn't let go of the wishbone and is catapulted over the rig. This can pull the mast foot out of the board, so it is imperative that it is leashed. Special care should be taken when wearing a harness. If you don't unhook, cannonading into the mast could break it, or knock you out. Alternatively, if you end up with the rig on top of you, the harness line has a nasty habit of taking a couple of turns round the hook, and it becomes difficult to escape from under the water. A V-shaped hook will help prevent this, but it is always advisable to have a quick release buckle so that you can get the harness right off in a hurry.

than technique to stay on your board. Constant bucking and changes in speed over waves threatens to throw you off balance. It is then that the right choice of rig, and a board equipped with footstraps that anchor your feet against the gusts, extend your ability to sail into the most difficult weather.

Capsize Falls

The capsize fall is caused by the daggerboard – and your technique.

As the board gathers speed it begins to aquaplane on its daggerboard. It rises up like a hydrofoil until it balances precariously, with the thrust from the mast foot pushing the board over to leeward. Suddenly it will say 'No more!', and flip up and over on its side.

Reaching

The reaches are the best fun. The board really gets up and goes, and it's all spray and excitement.

Bearing Off

Bearing off from a beat to a reach requires a different technique, depending on what sort of board you are sailing.

On a flat board you must steer it round with the rig. Rake it forward, sheet in (and out so you're not thrown off balance), crouch down a little for stability, and push with your front foot if necessary. That way the board will soon bear off, but beware the catapult fall!

If you have footstraps, it's a lot easier since your feet will be anchored against any sudden pull by the rig. Also, if you're going fast enough, you can help turn the board by banking it, pushing down the windward rail. (The opposite is the case on a strong wind board – you push down the lee rail.)

You can steer a round board very effectively with the feet. Push down the windward rail and it will bear off until you hop smartly back on to the centreline and straighten the board out.

Taking Off

Once on a reach, you should take off. In any wind over Force 3 it's the fastest point of sailing – the wind is on the beam for maximum drive.

As we've discovered, the most immediate problem is the capsize fall, solved by a storm or fully retractable daggerboard.

If you don't have either of these options (most likely if you're racing) you will have to pull the dagger – a tricky operation. You pause for a moment, holding the rig with the mast hand. You then bend down, pull the dagger, sling it over your arm, sheet in, and sail away.

Top: Pulling the dagger demands precise quick movements. It becomes difficult in waves – take care not to luff the board.

Above: Once the daggerboard is slung over your arm you can sheet in (keeping the mast well to windward) and sail away.

The trick is not to think too much. As soon as the dagger is removed, the board becomes markedly less stable ... so you've just got to get on and do it without thinking about it. As soon as you're under way, the board will be steady as a rock.

You can carry the dagger on either arm, but if it's the sheet arm you may need to cradle it in your

crotch so that it doesn't skip along the surface of the water.

Weight Distribution

This is important on the reach. You must keep the nose of the board well up so it won't submarine when it accelerates, and keep it steering straight with your feet – on a round board you'll need to dance a constant jig to try to keep it level and prevent it heading up or bearing off. The stronger it blows, the further outboard your feet need to be, but there comes a point when your heels dig in the water and send up a shower of spray, so you need to shift your feet inboard once again.

Bearing Off on to the Run
The technique is the same as for bearing off on to a reach – but it's even less fun. At least on the reach the rig is pulling, but when going on to the run, there comes a horrible moment when the wind goes behind, and the sail stops sucking as the laminar flow ceases. If you continue to pull, you'll fall in, so transfer your weight inboard pretty smartly, and get behind the sail, standing two square in your new running stance.

Above: Easy reaching on a *Windglider* with the daggerboard pulled. Many novices don't think it worth the effort of risking a fall to bend down and pull it, but without it the board is transformed and becomes a lot more stable to sail. However, if you race, it is worth practising with the dagger right down (sometimes you can't pull it).

Running

Running is the nightmare of all windsurfers.

With the wind right behind, you just can't lean back and enjoy yourself, but need to pursue a wobbly and precarious course, with no stability on either side.

In theory you need never run at all. You could close reach all the time (and never even have to beat), but in reality you will get caught out – perhaps being swept upwind by a benevolent tide – and of course, if you race, you'll have to do it all the time.

The technique is similar to running in light weather, except that now the rig is pulling a lot harder, and things are happening a great deal faster. You can't see the gusts (or the competitors) coming up behind you, but you need to be on your guard, ready to hop to the back of the board, pulling at the rig with all your might.

Whether it's flat or round, the board will be very prone to steer according to its shape, shooting off in one direction or the other rather more rapidly than you would like. Either way you may fall in, or collide with another board.

Enemies
There are two major enemies. The first is:

The daggerboard
From down there in the depths, the daggerboard will decide to take control of your board as soon as you turn on to a run.

You should get rid of it as soon as possible – either pull it or retract it, but remember that if it only folds back flush with the bottom of the board, that is not enough, and it will still want to steer you all over the place when it blows hard.

Once you have got rid of it the board will behave a lot better. It will be more stable, and if you don't

Running or broad reaching on an extreme strongwind board, most of the steering is done with the feet and weight distribution – the rig becomes secondary to the manoeuvrability of the board.

fall off, the next set of problems won't crop up until you decide you want to use the daggerboard once again!

The second enemy is:
Waves
Running through waves can be an extremely unpleasant experience. Strangely enough, it's better if the wind is reasonably strong, as this at least gives you something to brace yourself against. If it is fitful, you don't know where you are and soon become prone to the most terrible wobbles.

If you can't handle it, you must try getting your weight lower and consequently rocking the boat less. (Some of the round racing boards tried a hollowed-out canoe-style hull, so that the sailor could get his weight lower.) Try going down on

one knee, with the other leg spread-eagled behind you. It's uncomfortable, but it may work, and at least in this stance you can jump to your feet fairly rapidly.

If that's no good, try sitting down on the back end of the board, with the rig pulled down over your head. You'll get your weight very low for stability, and cut the amount of sail exposed to the wind, but will be a little stuck for steerage. If rocking the rig from side to side doesn't have a quick enough effect, you can always drop a leg over the side to slow the board down and slew it round.

Sitting will get you downwind, although it might be a rather slow passage. However, whichever way you do it, don't fall off! It's a hell of a job getting going again, as you've got to find your board, gingerly raise the rig (no daggerboard remember), and then try and bear it away on the direction of a broad reach before starting off and getting back on to the run. This is fine for superhuman windsurfers, but for the rest of us, it takes a long time.

Gybing

Surprisingly, gybing is nothing like as difficult as running – perhaps it's the realisation that you're getting off the run!

If you have steady nerves, you can gybe with the board running fast – if you haven't, you can always slow it down by standing on the back end so that the stern digs in and begins to drag.

You push the rig over to windward, crouching down with a little pumping of the sheet hand for stability. Pushing down on the windward rail the board will turn fast, but don't do anything until you are well through the eye of the wind – just right for a broad reach on the other tack. At this point, grab the mast just below the wishbone with your sheet hand. Take your mast hand off, the rig flips round, and hey presto, you can grab the new windward wishbone.

There are many variations on the strong wind gybe – if you want to know more about them, see pages 114–123.

If All Else Fails

Getting downwind on a tippy round board can be a real problem. Unless you have got the knack of steering the thing with your feet, you'll be falling off every other minute and getting increasingly tired and unhappy. There is one very slow but effective option. Simply let the rig blow in front of you like a flag, and with luck it will bring you home. If you can't manage that, you'd better ask for a lift – ask any windsurfer and he will tell you that ignominy is the better part of valour when there's tea waiting at home.

Above: Standing right on the back of the board – note the feet keeping balance!

Below: In very difficult conditions you can try lying on the board, but steering is difficult.

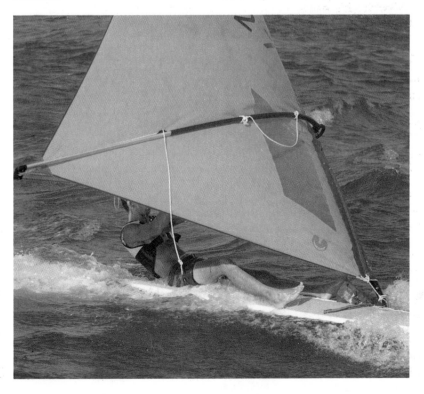

The Harness

It was the Hawaiians, led by Larry Stanley, who invented the harness in the mid seventies, and if they had patented it they would have made a fortune. As it is, windsurfers have a lot to be thankful for. Whereas the sport used to depend largely on strength – roughly translated into how long you could bear to hang on for – you can now hook in, hang on, and go for miles.

This is because your back is taking the strain from the sail, rather than your arms which now simply control which way the rig is pointing.

Technique

Before you use a harness you should be a proficient sailor in strong winds – otherwise, what would you do if your harness or harness lines broke when you were out sailing? Also you still need some muscle, and it is good to develop your forearms by using a harness as little as possible when it is not blowing so hard.

The harness lines should be pre-stretched terylene of around 5 mm diameter. They should be more or less 130 mm long, depending on whether you prefer them long or short.

You can simply tie them to the boom, or use custom-made tabs to hold the ends in place. Either way, they should only move when you want them to.

Try using a harness on dry land first. You need to hook in on the middle of the harness line, which will be about equal to the CE of the sail. Your hands should fall near each end of the line.

Obviously, the lines will need adjusting according to wind conditions. If it is blowing harder, you will want to shift them back along the wishbone to find the new CE.

When you are out on a board,

Top: The harness should give maximum support to the rib-cage, which is compressed, and the back from the shoulders to the waist. It should be a tight, but comfortable fit, with foam padding.

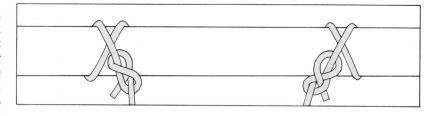

Above: The harness lines can be tied to the wishbone. You take a turn, and then tie a figure-of-eight knot around the line for it to slip through and tighten on. Tape on the wishbone will stop it sliding.

there is a knack in getting used to a harness. Come on to a close reach, dip your knees, and at the same time pull the wishbone sharply towards you to flip the harness line into the hook.

Once you have got the hook in, lean back and take your weight on the harness . . . you'll find it's pure luxury!

You need to take care. If the rig pulls hard, you go with it, so you have to be aware of gusts, controlling the incidence of the rig with your hands, and sheeting out or banking it to windward as necessary. If you really can't control it, you'll have to get unhooked or go with it.

The beats are relatively easy to predict and control when using a

Above: The alternative to tying is a tab. You can get Velcro ones which are very easy to use.

The sailor dips his knees and pulls the wishbone towards him with a sharp jerk to swing the line . . .

. . . the hook catches, and he leans back to take his weight on the line, his hands on the wishbone.

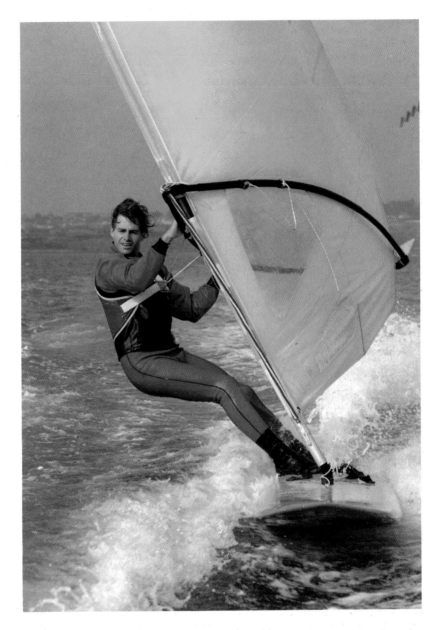

Above: Perfect harness technique demonstrated by Ken Winner. His back takes the strain, while his hands control the rig, and his feet control the board. This technique is taken to its ultimate conclusion railing a round board upwind. The upper part of the body stays rigidly hooked in, while the legs and feet do all the work, controlling just how much the board is allowed to rail.

harness, but the reach is more difficult – if you catapult and you're hooked in, you can go head over heels and cause a lot of damage. On the run it is never wise to hook in, however tired you are.

If you come off when hooked on, the harness line has a nasty habit of taking a couple of turns round the hook. If you're under the sail and disorientated, getting unhooked can quickly become a frightening experience. A V-shaped hook is unlikely to tangle, but you should always wear a harness that has a quick release buckle so that you can take it off in a hurry if necessary.

A harness should give maximum support to the whole of your back and rib cage. It should be well padded, and either have a back pack or a pocket for carrying spare harness lines. Ideally it should have buoyancy, though few harnesses are designed to float you face upwards if you are knocked out.

Getting Fit

To enjoy your windsurfing to the full it is worth making the effort to get fit for the job. Windsurfing is in in itself marvellous exercise, and the more you do the fitter you will become, but as with skiing you should try to get in reasonable shape for your board in the first place.

Cold weather saps energy very quickly in a strong wind. Before considering how to improve your muscles, you should look at two points:

1. Diet

The heavier you are the more weight you and your board have to carry. You get more tired than someone who is lighter, and your board travels more slowly. Therefore, watch your weight!

However, you need immediate energy and to this end sugar is your most effective form of nourishment. Make sure you eat properly before sailing, and if you are going out for a long time take some glucose tablets or even chocolate in your back pack.

2. Clothing

There is always the danger that your body will get progressively colder while you are out on the water. When you are sailing along in a strong breeze, you are using enough energy and pumping enough blood to keep warm, but once you stop, the cold sets in and you become less able to cope with the conditions.

You may be waiting for the start of a race, with the cold wind cutting down your body temperature, or you may fall off into cold water. Either way you must start exercising to keep the blood going. If you are unable to sail, sit on the board and do any exercise you can – twisting the body, shaking the wrists, and waving your arms like windmills over your head.

Strengthening the hands for the wishbone. Simply try to pull your clasped hands apart.

Strengthening hands. Squeezing a tennis ball is remarkably effective – and tiring!

Strengthening arms and back. Press-ups are a particularly effective form of torture.

Strengthening arms and back. Push hard in a doorway, and try to emulate Samson.

Strengthening arms and back. Pull-ups on a bar. Test the structure before you start.

Strengthening back and legs. Lie on your front and lift both ends, without cheating. This is also very unpleasant.

Strengthening back and arms. Don't lift your legs or you'll send the chair flying. Just try to lift your front half.

Strengthening back and legs. This one is not so difficult, but of course not as effective. It's the nasty ones that count.

Strengthening arms, back and legs. Raise your legs and stretch out your arms to meet them. This ends your daily routine.

So, be very careful about your clothing. It must keep you warm, but without promoting cramp by constricting your forearms.

Exercising
When you start windsurfing, most of your strength loss is in your hands and forearms. Until you have mastered harness technique (pages 92–93) the hands continuously clasp the wishbone, while the forearms carry the full weight of your body – the heavier you are, the stronger they must be.

The thighs, legs, and feet come under greater strain as your windsurfing becomes more advanced. Both roundboards and footstraps allow the sailor to control the direction of the board with his body rather than with the rig. With the roundboard he will constantly need to control the angle of rail with his legs – with footstraps his feet twist, push, and pull in the straps to steer the board.

You will benefit from visiting a gymnasium. Weightlifting strengthens the arms and the back, while bicycle machines and exercises will strengthen you from the waist down. Serious swimming is also very beneficial, but if you would rather make do at home, the exercises on these pages will help. These exercises should be done an increasing number of times each day. They are intended for both sexes and all ages, but if you're still not sure if you qualify, it may be wise to check with your doctor.

Top Techniques
from the Champions

When it comes to advanced techniques, we need the champions to explain how they do it. All day and every day they sail in the best places with the latest in boards and equipment to maintain their expertise.

However, given time and practice, any windsurfer can learn their tricks and techniques, whether they relate to racing in a World Championship, jumping in the waters off Hawaii, or designing and building a board from a foam core.

Racing with Karl Messmer

Swiss born Karl Messmer has won major regattas and events worldwide. His trophies include World and European titles in the Windsurfer, Mistral and Open Class.

Messmer has been involved with the design and development of boards since he first began to work full time in windsurfing in 1978. After teaching windsurfing in Spain, followed by a stint as a sail maker, Messmer joined Mistral in order to promote their boards worldwide and help with the production of new models. He worked closely with Chief Designer Ernstfried Prade on the very successful Mistral M1 and Takeoff.

Messmer's home is within easy reach of Lake Garda in northern Italy, the windsurfing mecca of central Europe. He reckons to get out

Karl Messmer: Swiss born *Open Class*, *Windsurfer*, and *Mistral* World Champion.

on the water most days in order to keep fit. He believes that sailing is more use than physical fitness training routines.

Success

To succeed as a regatta sailor requires dedication, and the standard is so high that Messmer reckons it is essential to have a job connected with windsurfing – only that way can you get the necessary time, expenses, and equipment to spend all the time training, racing, and travelling. No sailor has yet become rich by windsurfing, but some make a good living from it.

Messmer rates the single greatest problem for the regatta sailor as stress, which particularly affects younger, less experienced sailors. They can win a single race through instinctive ability, but it takes self-discipline and a cool temperament to have steady high placings throughout a series, and in the end that's what counts the most.

Types of Racing

The IYRU (International Yacht Racing Union) which is the governing body of international competitive sailing, reorganised 'Open Class' boards into three new Divisions in 1980, so that national sailing organisations could run official racing on their behalf.

The three Divisions are:
Division I
Series boards and prototypes with an absolute maximum hull thickness of 16.5 cm. Every board must be licensed by the national authority.
Division II
The construction class for production and prototype 'round boards', with a 22 cm maximum hull thickness. This was previously called IBSA Division I!
Division III
Open Class tandems.

Major Class Associations
The most important international class associations directly answerable to the IYRU are:

The International Windglider Class (IWGC).
The International Windsurfer Class Association (IWCA).
The International Mistral Competition Class (IMCO).
The International Board Sailing Association (IBSA).

The IYRU approve the internationally standardized regatta regulations of these associations. The one-design Mistral, Windglider and Windsurfer are also required to be constructed of the same material and to the same specification by all their licensed builders.

IWGC
The IWGC was founded on 11 March 1976, and four years later the IYRU chose the Windglider as the first Olympic class board, to be sailed in the Los Angeles 1984 Games.

The Windglider board is built of polyester and plastic, strengthened with glassfibre. When racing, it must be used with a daggerboard and a 6.3 sq m approved racing sail. Unusually, the use of harnesses is forbidden, and there is only one weight group.

IWCA
The IWCA is the oldest of all the class associations. They had a Windsurfer European and World Championship in 1973. Since that time there has been little basic change in the board: plastic rather than wood fittings; new daggerboard; better finish; and varying amounts of buoyancy and rocker.

The Windsurfer is manufactured under licence to Hoyle Schweitzer in various countries – the USA, the Netherlands (the biggest), Australia, and Japan. It is moulded in a polyethylene skin and foamed.

During racing, the standard Windsurfer 5.6 sq m sail must be used, together with the plastic daggerboard and aluminium wishbone. Harnesses are permitted.

At international championships there are four weight groups (Light; Light-Medium; Medium-Heavy; Heavy). There is also a separate class for women.

Right: The first reach during the *Open Class* World Championship held in Guadeloupe in the French Caribbean.

IMCO

IMCO was founded in 1978, the youngest of these organisations. However it has become established very quickly. The great advantage of the Mistral board is large volume (260 litres) and light weight (18 kg), which gives reasonably close racing for heavy or light sailors.

The Mistral Competition one-design board is made of epoxy resin, and when racing can use a combination daggerboard which can be shortened from full length to storm length. The standard sail is 6.3 sq m, but smaller Mistral sails can be used to suit the conditions. The harness is allowed, and at international championships there are three weight groups, including one for women.

IBSA

The Open Class Division is the internationally recognised 'round board' class, which was developed for the IYRU by IBSA.

IBSA itself was founded in Sardinia in 1978, and its first Open Class World Championship was held in Guadeloupe in 1979, followed by Israel and Florida.

Division II boards are used solely for regattas, and specifically made and designed for triangle racing. The kudos and publicity that result from winning these events is very important, and with the chance to participate with prototypes, major manufacturers provide heavy financial backing for their teams.

The Division II specifications have resulted in the standard round board. This should not weigh less than 18 kg; it should be no longer than 3.9 m; the maximum width is 62 cm with the middle height of the board 59 cm per 1.5 m; it should be no more than 22 cm thick at any point.

Two daggerboards (long and short) and two sails (standard and strong wind) can be used in a regatta. Carbon fibre or Kevlar are

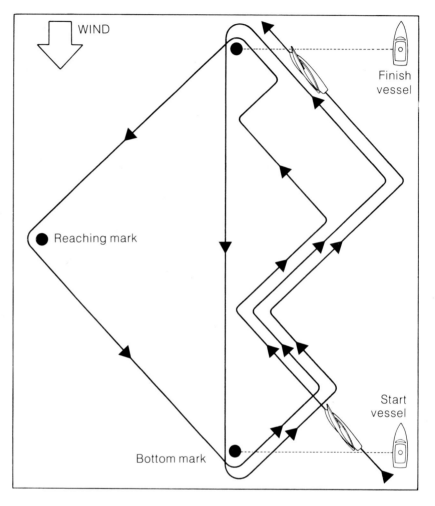

not allowed in a board's construction. The harness is allowed, and there are three weight groups, including one for women.

Triangle Racing

Triangle races have been adapted from the dinghy classes. The start is always into the wind, with three equal legs. First you sail upwind to Mark No. 1; then a close reach to gybe at Mark No. 2; on to a broader reach to Mark No. 3 (at the start line); the same upwind leg to No. 1; a run to No. 3; and finally again upwind to the finish line beyond No. 1.

The one-design classes, the Open Class, and the tandems, all use these triangles, with leg lengths of 1–2 km.

The Olympic triangle is used in most major regattas, and always works along the same principles.

The course is either a starboard hand course, or a port hand course, denoted by a green or red flag flown by the committee boat. The one illustrated here is port hand – ie all the marks are to port.

The first leg is a beat directly into the wind. The boards then bear away on a reach to the reaching mark, where they gybe on to the opposite reach. They then round the bottom mark and beat up to the top once again.

The next leg is a dead run back down to the bottom mark. Finally they beat up to the finish which is close to the top mark (and can be confused with it).

Above: Windsurfer class boards during their 1979 World Championship in Greece.

When there are a large number of identical one-design boards, a 'gate' is sometimes used at the start. Rather than every individual jockeying for position, a single board sails across the fleet at full speed on one tack. Every other board has to sail round its stern on the other tack in order to start, guaranteeing that everyone starts equally.

Left: Gybing around the mark during the Open Class World Championship held in Israel in 1980. The sailor is Thomas Staltmaier, who won the heavyweight class on a Mistral M1.

Funboard Racing

Funboard racing is very different from the normal funboard strong wind type surf-sailing. The boards are built specially for regattas such as the Pan Am Cup, which are only held if the wind blows over Force 4. They have courses with a lot of reaching; long distance races; and ins-and-outs.

The best boards for these events are 3.6–3.9 m long, with flat hull shapes and retracting daggerboards. On the whole, the regulations that govern these boards are varied, and have nothing to do with any international body or the IYRU.

Funboard racing is far more entertaining for the spectators. It is easier to make out what is happening, and if there is surf it is even more spectacular.

It is also a lot of fun for the competitors. These events demand excellent technique and very careful board preparation. The competitors can race fairly in strong winds, when no-one can pump. The problem is, however, that it is necessary to travel a long way to those places that have constant favourable (Force 4+) conditions.

A typical funboard race will have four marks set in a square, with two long parallel reaching legs, and two short parallel upwind legs. First there is a short upwind leg to Mark No. 1; then a long reach of up to 2 km to Mark No. 2, around which you gybe. You then reach back to No. 1; slalom down to the start (Mark No. 3); another reach straight across to No. 4; upwind to No. 2; back across to No. 1; and slalom down to the finish at No. 3.

Pan Am Racing

The Pan Am Cup is held at Kailua on the island of Oahu, Hawaii, and is designed around the special conditions encountered there.

The regatta consists of triangle racing, long-distance racing, and ins-and-outs, all of which contribute a percentage towards the final result.

In themselves the courses are nothing special, but they are made more difficult by the strong winds (Force 4+), the big Pacific swell, the surf breaking on the coral heads, and the jagged coral islands that are used as rounding marks. It all means that competitors must have absolute control over their boards, and be in peak physical condition.

The racing demands constant speed rather than tactical ability. The boards are slow to tack due to their large skeg areas, and the wind is constant, so there is no need to sail the type of race where every windshift is exploited. Board handling is the main secret of winning, and this is why the Hawaii based sailors have a marked advantage in this event.

For security and safety reasons, only 60 finalists are allowed. The boards are either 'anything goes', or are built to the Division II rules, with footstraps, though no one is too fussy about measurements.

Competitors who do well at this event are unofficially hailed as the best windsurfers in the world – it is the most difficult that I know of.

(*Editor's note: Karl Messmer was fifth at his first attempt in 1981.*)

Pan Am Triangles

Each leg is long – approximately 3 km, and there is no running leg.

Pan Am Long Distance

Approximately 40 km through big seas and breaking surf, with the markers being rock outcrops (Birdshit Island, as it is inelegantly referred to by windsurfers, and Flat Island).

Pan Am Ins-and-outs

A short upwind leg; reaching out and back through the surf; then a short run to the finish. This event is sailed in groups on a knock-out system.

Above: Start of a Pan Am Cup race during the 1981 series. Note the variety of boards and the differences in rigs and sails – with a relatively light wind (just about Force 4) some sailors have opted for large area fatheads.

Right: The top mark during the famous ins-and-outs of 1980, when it blew hard all the time. Note the breaking surf and remember that there is an unpleasant coral lee shore (Flat Island) for anyone who comes off and can't handle it.

During this racing the boards were going so fast that their main problem was not to get airborne (which would only lose them speed). Note the board on the right just starting to take off over a breaking crest. Seconds later it inadvertently looped the loop.

Preparation

Even when they involve going through the surf, European regattas are generally held around buoys, mainly using the racing triangle.

Starting Procedure
Before the first race of a regatta, the competitor should have full knowledge of the starting procedure and the course – as well as having studied the detailed sailing instructions which are issued to all the participants.

It is essential not to make any mistakes. Work out what is required so that you can't get confused, and make sure you know by heart every flag the starter boat is likely to fly: red for a starboard hand course; green for a port hand course; the 'Blue Peter' for five minutes to go; the race abandonment flag; the shortened course flag; the requirement to wear a life jacket – and many more.

It is also necessary to learn all the right-of-way rules and rule infringements. For example, a competitor who touches a buoy on his way round it must go round it again, avoiding all other boards, or he will be disqualified.

Similarly, if a competitor first touches another board and then acknowledges he is wrong, he can avoid disqualification by executing a 720 degree turn – turning his board twice round beneath his feet, and once again avoiding all other boards.

The Board
It is essential for the underside of the board to have a reasonably smooth finish. However it shouldn't be too smooth. You should aim for a mat finish which will allow a thin layer of water to adhere to it. This is advisable since friction is least when water flows past water.

Top: In the *Open Classes* all boards need to be scrutinized and measured before they can race in a major championship.

Above: Sails need to be carefully treated. These *Open Class* sails are dried out and carefully stored between every race.

A 400 grade wet-and-dry sandpaper will achieve the right result on a good surface, and will also get rid of wax and grease.

Daggerboard and Skeg
These should be prepared along the same principles as the hull. Particular care should be taken with a laminated ply daggerboard, since it will be prone to warping, swelling up, and distortion if it is incorrectly stored or not properly varnished or painted. Constant attention – sandpapering, filling, varnishing/paint-

ing – will be necessary to keep the leading edges in raceworthy condition.

Many Division 2 boards have a slot gasket to prevent water coming up through the daggerboard case. You should always check that this is working effectively, and is properly bonded in place. With constant use, it may need replacing several times a season.

Topsides
Grip on the deck of the board is very important in racing. Apart

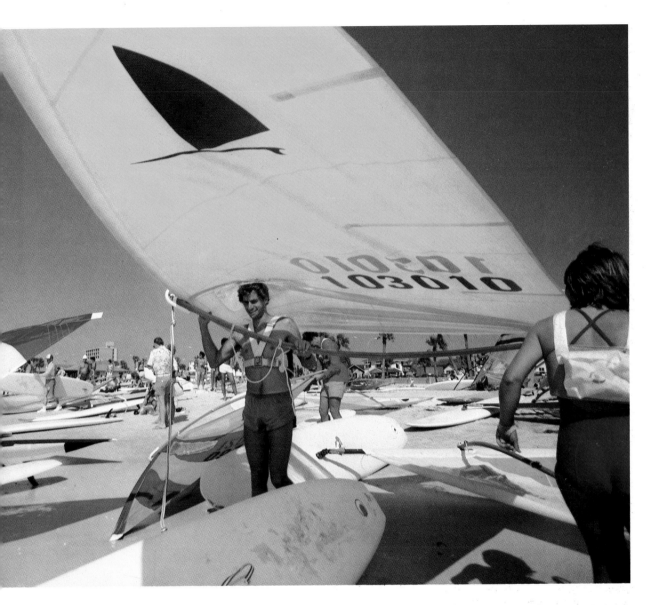

from choosing footwear which has a
suitable rubber compound, you can
improve the non-slip properties by
rubbing on special board wax. (Sex
Wax is a well-known brand!)

The Rig
If there's a choice, choose the right
rig for the conditions. With classes
such as the Windsurfer you are
stuck with the standard sail, but in
the Open Class you can go as small
as you like. If this enables you to
get round the course without falling
off, you'll probably get to the finish

before the guy who's fallen off half-
a-dozen times with a big sail.

Remember that where there is a
choice of sails you will probably be
limited to a total of two for use
throughout the regatta.

When you choose your sail, plan
for the series – not just the one race.

Other equipment
Some regatta organizers require
that you wear buoyancy aids.
Check this one out, or you could
get disqualified. In most cases a
buoyancy harness will suffice.

Above: Between races check that
everything is right with your board
in plenty of time. Don't leave
anything to the last minute.

Finally, and most important,
you need a stopwatch with a 10
minute countdown. There was a
time when these were very expensive. However, the new generation
of digital quartz watches are ideal
for the purpose. They have multi-
functions, are relatively cheap, and
in most cases are sufficiently waterproof.

The Start

A race starts long before the starting gun is fired. So a competitor should not only be armed with theoretical and practical knowledge of the regatta he will be sailing, but must also find plenty of time to warm up and practice various manoeuvres. These will loosen the muscles, allowing maximum physical performance during the race, and preventing any likelihood of cramp, as well as awakening the sense of fine balance which is so important when sailing a round-board.

Getting out early brings many advantages. Wind and waves can be studied, and the tactical approach can be planned. Once the buoys are in position, there is also time to work out which is the best side of the course to sail up.

Another advantage of getting to the start line early is that the competitor can try out his tack for the first leg. (Remember that a stopwatch is indispensible!)

In many ways, the start is the most important part of the whole race. At no other time will the competitors be so densely concentrated in one area.

Start Signals

Make sure you understand the signals before you go out to the start line. These are: a preliminary signal ten minutes before the start; another signal five minutes before the start; a preparatory one minute signal; then the start. If the start is unruly, the Race Officer may introduce the One or Five Minute Rules to discipline the field. These rules forbid boards to cross the line from any direction within the allotted time, and may lead to disqualification – they must be learnt by heart!

The first thing to remember at the start is not to take any position on the line which restricts your

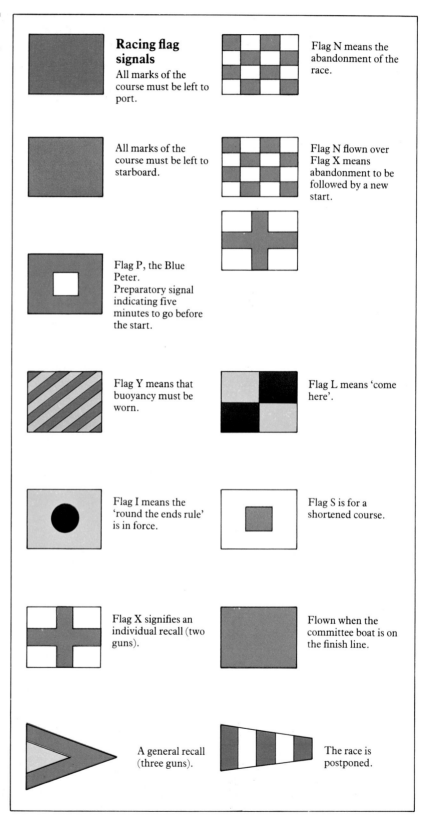

Racing flag signals
All marks of the course must be left to port.

All marks of the course must be left to starboard.

Flag P, the Blue Peter. Preparatory signal indicating five minutes to go before the start.

Flag Y means that buoyancy must be worn.

Flag I means the 'round the ends rule' is in force.

Flag X signifies an individual recall (two guns).

A general recall (three guns).

Flag N means the abandonment of the race.

Flag N flown over Flag X means abandonment to be followed by a new start.

Flag L means 'come here'.

Flag S is for a shortened course.

Flown when the committee boat is on the finish line.

The race is postponed.

freedom of movement (because of the other boards around you). You must be able to pump away fast. Thus:

1. You must be on the right part of the line with regard to the tactical requirements of the first leg.

2. You must cross the line with sufficient speed at the starting signal. This is only possible if there is enough space on your leeward side (2–4 m) to bear away and pick up speed. It can be done, however, by a competitor who knows the rules and keeps a cool head.

3. Go for speed first – the correct course comes second.

4. Lack of confidence may make you look back as you leave the line – and then you may as well go back to the start position!

In Conclusion

A good regatta surfer is one who possesses a high degree of concentration, who has strong nerves, and who has perfect control over the board. These factors are imperative in the chaos of the start line, as is a knowledge of the rules.

Start Positions

The choice of where to start depends on whether the start line is biased to the left or right hand side of the course, although the wind never blows constantly from any one direction. Even so, the sailor should try to decide which end of the line is nearest to the first mark. If there is no bias, it is probably best to start in the middle.

The Right Hand Side

Many competitors opt to start on the right hand side. As everyone wants to get the optimum windward placing, this approach will normally only succeed in very small regatta fields. It also becomes immensely difficult in a strong wind, when it is hard to keep the board in

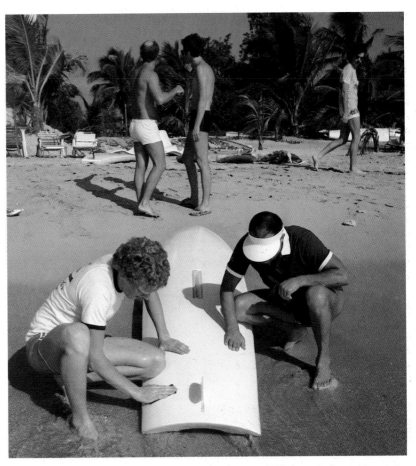

Above: The bottom is scrupulously prepared before every race. This is a *Windglider* prototype.

Below: When all the boards are the same make (Windsurfers here) mark which one is yours.

STARTING TACTICS

WIND

A perfectly laid starting line which has a slight disadvantage at the starboard committee boat end, giving boards some incentive to start down to leeward.

A very biased line with the port end much closer to the windward mark. If it's not too crowded, port tack boards could clear the fleet from this end of the line.

A favourite tactic as boards wait to dive round the stern of the committee boat and get the best windward berth. Success depends on timing and board control.

GATE START

WIND

The sailor chosen as Pathfinder sails across the fleet close-hauled and as fast as he can. When the Gate Boat following him signals the start of the race, any board crosses the starting line when it crosses under the Gate Boat's stern. The Pathfinder must start by gybing, and then also cross under its stern.

Pathfinder

Gate Boat

position – tucked in to windward of the fleet. You are always making leeway.

The best way to get the windward position is to sail round from behind the Committee Boat, and drift into position, at the same time killing the sail. This manoeuvre is very difficult and needs careful practice – remember that you have no right of way over other boards that are already on the line – just in the place you want!

You have to work out whether you want to be right up to windward – and hemmed in by all those wanting to be in the same position – or are better off starting a little further down to leeward so that you can sail free and fast.

If you have not succeeded in getting in the first line of boards, at least you have right of way over port hand boards.

The right hand side has many disadvantages. Even if it is the biased side of the course, so many sailors start there from habit and lack of imagination that you may get held up on your way to the first mark by their backwinding and

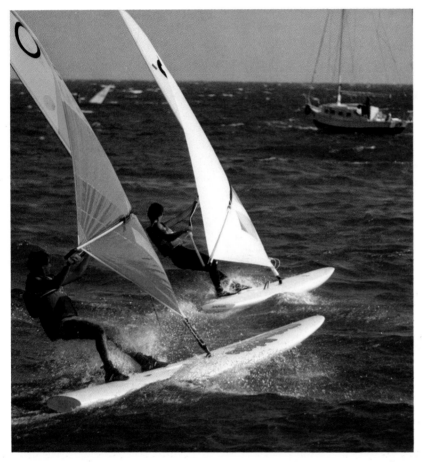

Above: If you are not sure about the performance of your board check it out with a friend.

Below: Many arrive at the start line late. It always pays to leave before the main rush.

everyone's lack of manoeuvrability. Those that cannot start at top speed soon get into a hopeless position, and fall back out of contention.

Therefore, unless it is immensely biased, try starting farther down to leeward on the line.

The Left Hand Side

Starting down this end, you need different tactics to get away at full speed. As this end normally has a small bias built in by the Committee Boat to compensate for the leeward position, you can get away immediately on the starboard tack, taking great care not to get pushed off the end of the line before it is time to start.

The initial reward in starting down at the port end of the line will be a free wind and room to manoeuvre – after that it will depend on whether the wind suddenly decides to head the boards on the starboard tack, or free them, and you should have worked this out in your pre-regatta research.

Once you need to tack on to port, always make sure that there is a big gap in the starboard tack boards to make it worth your while.

Port Tack Start

To succeed with this start, the sailor must have enough room to cross the line at full speed at the port end of the line, and clear the mass of boards coming at him on the starboard tack. It demands precise timing and judgement, because if the starboard boards force him to tack, all may be lost.

Starting in the Middle

When you start in the middle, the boards on either side of you will determine your tactics. Luff the ones to windward, giving yourself enough room to leeward to bear off and hit the line at full speed. (Remember that on a long line there is always an immense sag, with boards two or three lengths behind the line.)

The Race

Windward Legs

When you have left the start line, it is extremely important to choose the right initial tacks. Your tactics should be determined by your position relative to other boards and by wind shifts.

The overriding consideration as the start gun goes is to get clear so that you have total freedom of movement as to where you want to go. Boards to windward and to leeward cause adverse backwinding and get in your way – in this situation you must either free off and foot through to leeward, or tack if you can find a gap in the mass of boards sailing on the starboard tack. Once you're free of this massive interference from other boards, you are also free to choose your tacks.

In general, different tactics are demanded by inland waters and by the open sea. On inland waters you can expect constant wind shifts, which can make the greatest difference to victory or defeat. Therefore you must react instantly, by tacking on each wind shift. Only in this way will you make ground to windward at the fastest possible speed.

On the open sea it is rather different. There is usually a more constant wind, and speed differences between boards are far more likely to be influenced by sailing technique. The person who sails a board best through wind and waves sails fastest.

Of course, tactics also play their part. You should have precise knowledge of the tide – which way it is running and how fast. You should establish the likely weather pattern – will the offshore morning breeze turn onshore in the afternoon?

Sailing in waves demands great skill, particularly if the wind-blown waves are converging with the

natural swell, which will result in a very confused sea. In this case you should always sail free and go for speed, particularly if you are getting into troughs that are so deep that there is no wind.

Rounding the Windward Mark

Choosing the final beat up to the buoy is critical. The most common mistake is to tack too soon. The closer you get, the more you have to pinch up to windward, and the board loses power and speed. If there are other boards converging on the mark ahead of you, their turbulence will begin to affect your performance so that you are pointing five degrees below your desired course.

The result is that you find you cannot get round the mark, so that you need to put in another short

Above: A mass start to the Long Distance race during the 1979 Windsurfer World Championship. Long Distance races normally cover 20 miles or more, and if possible include a great deal of reaching. They frequently have a Le Mans start on the beach. The sailors line up with their boards at the water's edge, and when the gun goes, push them afloat, jump aboard, and sail off.

Right: Chaos, rounding a mark from the reach to the beat, during the Windsurfer World Championship held in the Bahamas in 1980. When a mass of overlapping boards converge on a mark, the outside ones have to give 'water', but chaos results when sailors drop their rigs or fall off – you must always avoid them.

tack. The closer you are to the mark, the more difficult this is because of the other boards. However, attempting to squeeze round the mark and accidentally hitting it should be avoided at all costs. You will have to round it again, avoiding all the other boards, and you will lose many places.

Therefore you should always choose your last beat when you are relatively close to the mark. You will be close enough to get it right ('overstanding' the mark so that you have to reach down on it also loses a lot of places). If you're on the port tack, you won't find a dense mass of starboard tack boards converging on the mark unless you are very close to it – and then you can ascertain whether the mark will be clear enough for you to round it on the port tack.

Reaches
If your course is not affected by waves or the tide, you should always aim to sail the direct course for the next mark.

Reaching through waves is a great experience which also gives a regatta sailor a big opportunity to enlarge his lead. However pumping is a problem which often results in lengthy protest meetings and eventual disqualification. The IYRU dictum is that there should be no pumping on the upwind legs, but on the reaches you can pump up to a maximum of three times to promote planing and surfing.

The reaching course involves a lot of snaking, as all wind and wave fluctuations should be used to keep top speed. It is always important to luff towards a wave, and then bear away and surf with it.

If you want to overtake other boards, you have to decide whether to overtake to windward or to leeward. You should always take into consideration how this will affect your position on rounding the mark – whether you will be inside or outside other boards.

You must also be very careful if you are sailing with the daggerboard withdrawn. Your board will be very prone to attack by boards with their daggerboards down, since they may be more manoeuvrable.

Runs

Many sailors underestimate the importance of runs, but there are tremendous opportunities to improve your position.

Here, more than at any other time, the boards behind can interfere with the wind of the leaders, and everyone should try to keep their wind clear.

You must also choose whether to head straight for the mark, or to try downwind tacking. If the wind is light, you're better off taking the shortest course, but with Force 4+ you can try very broad reaches on a number of tacks – even though you sail further, the speed difference may compensate.

If it's extremely windy, and there are big waves, you'll find downwind tacking is at its most effective. Increased pressure on the sail makes it easier for you to keep your balance, and you benefit from surfing down the wave faces.

Finish

Tactics at the finish are crucial. You must watch and cover your opponents all the time, without being taken in by a sham move. Try not to get too closely involved with another board – it will almost certainly lead to loss of overall places.

Watch out for any bias on the finish line. Theoretically it will be at 90 degrees to the wind, but in practice this is seldom the case – and crossing the right end of the line may win you the race.

Protests

Races can be won off the course, and a complete understanding of the racing rules is vital.

Sooner or later you will be involved in a protest if you aim to take your racing seriously. If the sailor in the wrong absolves himself by executing a 720 degree turn that is fine, but otherwise you must protest, remembering the following:

1. You must tell the other sailor you intend to protest. Cry 'Protest!' or '720!' If he then absolves himself, well and good.
2. If he doesn't, look for witnesses who can support your case.
3. Advise the committee boat whom you intend to protest.
4. When on land write down details and a diagram of your protest, quoting the relevant rule number. Deliver the protest to the race committee within the time limit.
5. Discuss the incident with your witnesses before they appear before the race committee.

Left: An upwind leg during the Open Class World Championship held in Guadeloupe in 1979. With a big Olympic course, the boards soon become very spaced out, and it is difficult to establish positions until they round the top mark of the course. This makes triangle racing a poor spectator sport which is seldom televized. All the speed and drama is lost on the screen.

Above: Going from a reach to a reach as the boards gybe round the mark during the same race. When a lot of boards converge on a mark at the same time, there is a great deal of place swopping. Many have their wind affected by the boards behind, and it frequently pays to keep well clear and sail round the outside unless you are well established close in.

If you are protested:

1. If you know you are in the wrong, avoid being disqualified with a 720.

2. If you reckon you are in the right, look out for witnesses.

3. Check that the protesting boardsailor has followed the correct procedure.

4. Check the relevant racing rule and prepare your defence with help from witnesses. Remember that there are exceptions to every rule, and don't assume your case is hopeless. Protests are unpleasant, but they are frequently fought on psychological grounds and have unexpected outcomes.

Unfortunately some regattas get bogged down in protests to the extent where it becomes unsportsmanlike and undesirable.

Wave Sailing with Fraser Black

You can ride and jump waves with almost any board and rig – but with limited success. However in the past decade there have been many design and detail improvements to make things easier.

Initially installing a smaller daggerboard and footstraps may suffice. However as your ability develops, so will the need for more specialized gear.

The Rig

Mast, sail, booms and universal joint are subject to high stress in wave sailing. By reducing the overall dimensions to a minimum, the rig can be made more manoeuvrable, robust, and efficient, but few manufacturers produce equipment with the stresses of surf sailing in mind – you should be sure the gear you get has been tested in these conditions.

Sails

Wave sailors generally choose sails of 5.1 sq m and under. The reason is that any area greater than this offers relatively little more power, while severely limiting manoeuvrability and control. A high clew with the booms aligned at right angles to the mast is a virtual must for wave sailing, in order to keep the end of the wishbone clear of the water. (If you don't want to buy a new sail, a sail maker can easily recut the foot of an old one.)

When you're buying new, look for favourable points in the sail. It should have a long, low window filling most of the area beneath the booms so that you can see the waves; a flattish foil with a maximum depth of no more than 10% of the chord; and a flat rather than hooked leech to allow air to flow freely out of the sail. Dacron cloth of either 4.2 or 3.8 oz is best suited to waves, and will last longer than Mylar.

A good controllable sail maintains its Centre of Effort in a fairly constant position forward of the

Above: Fraser Black comes from a Scottish family who are notably fond of the water. His father Alastair has taken most of the photographs for this book, and his brother Ken is one of the leading British windsurfer sail makers.

Fraser moved to Hawaii in 1979 to study wave sailing, and finished 4th overall in the 1980 Pan Am Cup. He has been closely associated with shaper and designer Brian Hinde, races in the Mistral Team alongside Robbie Naish, and is regarded as one of the foremost wave experts in the world.

midships point along the booms. The way to test this is to sheet in normally, and then gradually bring your hands close together. If control can be maintained when they are touching, then you have found an ideal sail, while a sail that leaves you struggling, pushing and pulling when your hands are shoulder width apart is thoroughly unsuited to wave sailing.

In order to permit the use of shorter booms while maintaining

sail area, a number of designs incorporating battens have pre-empted the popular pin head and straight leech sails. Some of these designs have been properly developed and tested, while others are mere gimmickry. If possible select proven designs from a reliable sailmaker, and try as many sails as possible in order to find out which ones suit you and the conditions best. Remember that as your abilities develop, so will your requirements in sails alter.

Masts

Of the scores of masts broken in the surf each year, most could be saved if the downed sailor guided his mast tip or wishbone end into the oncoming wave, holding it submerged as the wave struck. This is not always possible, and there are other reasons for breakages such as shore breaks and wipe outs.

Epoxy and glassfibre masts are still preferred to alloy, with medium flex characteristics being more resilient than stiffness. A soft mast won't give the sail sufficient support to hold its shape.

Once you have found a good mast, it is remarkable how long it stays in one piece, though reinforcement at the wishbone and base is a valuable precaution. The normal method is to use 4 in wide 6 oz glassfibre cloth soaked in resin.

Booms

The standard length wishbone for wave sailing is two metres or 2.1 m maximum. For winds of 30 knots + you may use one as short as 1.7 m.

The reasons for this trend to shortness are many: trimming the sail becomes much less effort and thus the rig responds instantly; the wishbone can be kept clear of the

Right: A clean jump with a tail first landing at the steepest part of the wave, which is anticipated perfectly to avoid it breaking over the nose of the board.

board, laying the calf on the deck. Now bend at the waist and bring hips as close to the board as possible. Use your back leg to propel your torso up out of the water. Thrust hips and solar plexus forward and up over the board as you sheet in and accelerate forward on to a beam reach.

If you feel more in control with your front leg in the water and back leg on the board, by all means reverse the legs.

It is vital to master this technique before you think of sailing a short board in severe waves. If you can't water start and gybe, you'll be lucky if you and the remains of your board get washed up on the beach after an hour or two in the water. If you're unlucky. . . .

Initially there is often difficulty getting close enough to the board to get either leg anchored. To overcome this problem raise arms above head and lay prone on your back. Drawing the tail towards yourself is not possible – the fins resist the sideways motion – but instead draw your legs to the tail of the board by extending your front arm directly above your head. Once you have got a heel on the board, bending the knee hooks the board in close to the torso. Bend at the waist (still submerged) and allow the rig to become as upright as possible before using the wind to lever your body on to the board.

Another problem is being dragged forward as soon as the sail fills with wind. The rig then flips from the sailor's hands, and re-starting takes just that much longer.

This problem is caused by the rig beginning to move forward over the sailor's head. Pulling it back only forces more air into the sail, and the sailor must release the sheet hand to retrieve the situation. Unpowered, the rig can then be manoeuvred by the front hand alone.

Waterstarts

The most valuable technique used in surf is the waterstart. This energy-saving manoeuvre will aid greatly in recovering control quickly, and avoid excessive risk of rig damage.

10–15 knot winds are best suited to develop the technique. Ideally the board should be pointed directly toward the wind, with the mast lying in the water at right angles to the board, and clew downwind. If the clew is upwind, simply lift the boom end a little and allow water to drain off the sail over the mast. Lift the boom end higher, and if the wind is moderately strong it will flip the sail from your hand into the mast first position.

Swim or stand (if it's shallow) beside the booms in front of the mast. Grasp the mast above the booms and raise it slightly clear of the water. This will encourage wind to flow beneath the sail. Gradually

water will be displaced over the leech – swimming the mast forwards into the wind speeds up the process.

Ultimately the clew will rise free of the water. Swim beneath the sail to place the back hand on the boom. The front hand, still supporting the rig, can either grasp the boom in the regular position, or in lighter winds some way below the booms.

Sheeting in with the back hand bringing the clew almost to the water will lift the mast. Use the power from the rig to guide the board. Try to move close to the tail, and begin swinging the nose away from the wind by light sheet action. Take care to sheet in only enough to keep the sail above your head. Ease off if you are drawn upwind, or you will not be able to sustain control of the rig.

Swing the front leg up on to the

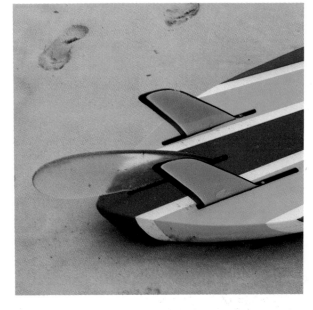

Conventional mast foot wells are being replaced by deck mounted fin boxes fitted with tracks which the rubber UJ can be attached to. This system developed by Mike Horgan and Peter Trombley allows fine tuning, but is not suited to floaters, as it is likely to lead to broken masts.

The fins can make or break a board. Kanger's cocks, donkey's ears, reverse foils and endless variations have established the validity of the conventional shape, though cavitation plates are sometimes valuable. If your board has a tail over 35 cm wide, a single fin is unlikely to be sufficient.

wave in tight situations, allowing the rider to manoeuvre closer to the critical section of the wave; the overall width of the wishbone can be reduced, allowing the sailor to be closer to the rig and in greater control – since the sail draught should not exceed 90% of the chord, a 2.25 m wishbone of 40 cm width should not interfere with sail shape. (Precise contouring of the booms to match the sail shape adds even more control over the trim of the rig.)

The boom ends should be compact, robust and functional. They should lock tight at the mast, preventing a loose and sloppy response due to rocking up and down. The clew end will strike the sea bottom frequently in shallow water wipe-outs, and a smooth profile will prevent it from catching on rock or coral. It is also less likely to cause any injuries to the sailor – from this point of view it is far better to do away with cleats and tie the outhaul with half-hitches at the clew end of the wishbone.

The Board

There are three basic categories of wave boards: the floater; semi-floater/marginal; and the sinker. As a sailor's ability advances he will progress through each of these.

Floaters are so named because they fully support the weight of the rig and rider. A floater over 2.75 m long can generally be tacked.

Marginals only partially support rig and rider when static. Pulling up the rig requires careful weight placement, and even so the board may be submerged during the procedure. Tacking will require lightning speed.

Sinkers do not support rig and rider in any substantial way, and therefore must be beach or water-started.

The volume of foam within a board determines how much weight it will support. Overall thickness

and deck/rail profiles are other major factors, as well as length, width and to a lesser degree board weight. General extremes of wave sailing sizes are: length 2 m to 3 m; max width 50 cm to 65 cm; nose width (30 cm back from the nose) 28 cm to 43 cm; tail width (30 cm up from the tail) 28 cm to 48 cm.

Wide Versus Narrow

Reducing width generally allows for more manoeuvrability. By retaining or even adding width, overall stability can be maintained. Generally, as a sailor improves, he will progress to narrower boards, and the loss in stability will go almost unnoticed.

The mean location of the widest point of the board is slightly forward of its middle. By moving it further forward the outline shape of the tail becomes straighter, and the effect is to improve board speed at the expense of manoeuvrability. Moving the wide point aft puts

The Carve Gybe

Gybing for many is an awkward and tricky operation, and the difficulties are often related to the 'unnatural' body language required to execute the transition. However nothing looks more fluid than a planing carve gybe.

Wavesailing boards behave like skis. Turns are carved by planting the inside rail, while with a 3.6 m board the reverse is normally true.

In order to practice carve gybes, a suitable board must be acquired. Try the following test to see how your board carves: planing on a close reach with your feet in the straps, depress the toes and lift the heel of your front foot. *Excellent response* throws you and the board into a sweeping curve away from the wind, while *average response* means that the board will turn gradually away from the wind with no rig movements apart from sheeting in — the former is unlikely to happen on anything except a sinker with a narrow tail. *Poor response* is when the rail submerges to leeward with no direction change.

Initiating the gybe is a combination of techniques. Start the turn as for the test **(1);** thrust the hips to the inside of the turn and incline and twist the upper body as a cyclist would **(2)** which means sheeting in, but don't drop the clew too low or you'll lose control with it jammed in the water. Pull back on the rig and put most weight on the back foot, which is pushing the inside rail. To get the board to carve tight you need to take your foot out of the back strap and put it close to the rail; when the board starts on a full downwind course, board speed and wind speed will be closely matched, and the rig will no longer perpetuate the carve. The momentum will carve the board through the eye of the wind, and then stall. To complete the gybe, slide the front foot back and the back foot forward, and depress the outside rail. The rig in the clew first position **(3)** requires a solid anchor with the clew hand. This technique will bring the board on to a close reach. To return from clew first, release the clew hand **(4)**, draw the mast forward as the rig revolves, release the mast hand from the boom and prepare to sheet in with both hands on the new gybe.

curve and hips into the outline shape of the tail. The planing area is increased allowing earlier planing, but maximum speed will be reduced by the resistance created by water being drawn into the more pronounced curve at the tail.

The wider the board the greater its planing surface, and in marginal conditions wide boards offer excellent performance. In higher winds their extra surface area will drag, and the tendency to bounce and skip will be much greater than with a narrower board, while responsiveness and turning ability will be lost.

Narrower tails extend the length of the planing surface, immersing more rail and thus increasing lateral resistance. The load on fins is thus reduced, while wide tails rely heavily on the fins to prevent sideslip, and are more prone to spin-out. The wider the tail, the more fins you need.

Scoop and Rocker

The standard formula for wave sailing is 2.5 cm of nose scoop for every 30 cm of length. Accentuating the curve in the last 15–30 cm helps 'pop' the nose out of the water should it ever bury. The curved nose flows into a relatively flat area around the mast foot from which speed is normally projected.

The last 45 cm of the board are critical to manoeuvrability. By adding tail rocker, turns are much more easily initiated. A standard amount of rocker on a 2.1–2.4 m board would be 3–4 cm measured from the fore and aft plane. Excessive tail rocker will slow the board.

Rail Profiles (*see diagram overleaf*)

The rails or outer extremities of the board accept and release water. Altering their shape vastly affects board handling and performance characteristics.

Low hard rails (1) release water from the tail area with minimum influence on water flow from the bottom of the board. The clean

release enhances speed, while in the nose this shape gives maximum life.

Drawbacks are the likelihood of tripping the board on the rail at the nose as it digs into the water: and the tail bouncing and skipping since the clean release fails to press the board to the water.

A full, soft rail is the opposite extreme (2). The effect of this is to slow the board by keeping it hugging the water. The smooth flowing curve encourages water to flow up around the rail, submerging the board, and the large volume of foam in the rail aids floatation and stability. The drawback is that jumps are sluggish as the board fights to stay with the water.

Between these two extremes

there are many compromises. The contemporary surfboard rail (3) is a good example, and a very popular choice. The maximum fullness of the rail is set at three-quarters depth, so that water tends to flow up around that first quarter to the fullest point, giving the board traction without sluggishness. The tucked underedge permits a clean release, so the rider gains straight line speed, while the fullness of the rail helps prevent skipping and sliding when he carves turns.

Finding the way back through a heavy shore break looks like a good time to damage a lot of equipment – beware the undertow when you hit the beach.

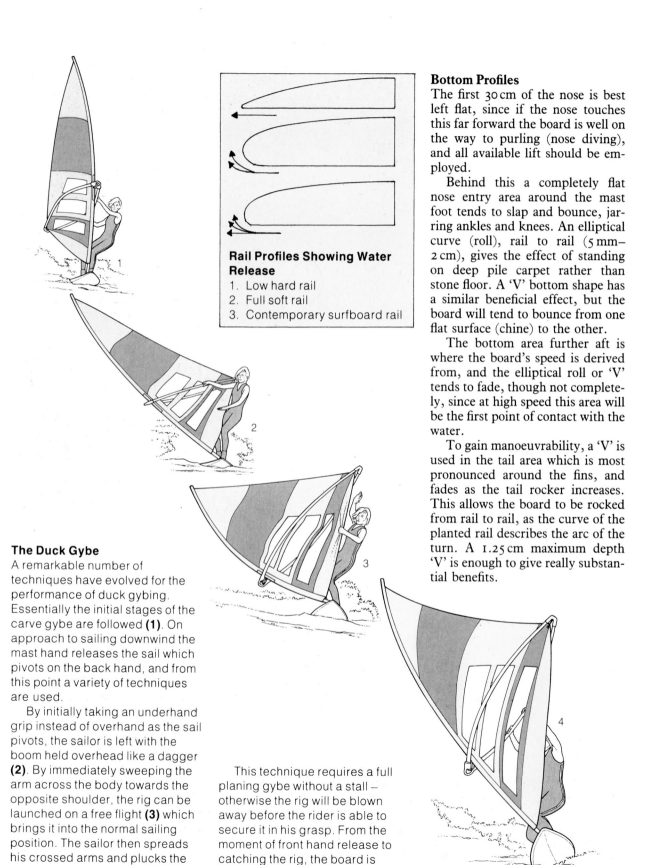

Rail Profiles Showing Water Release
1. Low hard rail
2. Full soft rail
3. Contemporary surfboard rail

Bottom Profiles

The first 30 cm of the nose is best left flat, since if the nose touches this far forward the board is well on the way to purling (nose diving), and all available lift should be employed.

Behind this a completely flat nose entry area around the mast foot tends to slap and bounce, jarring ankles and knees. An elliptical curve (roll), rail to rail (5 mm– 2 cm), gives the effect of standing on deep pile carpet rather than stone floor. A 'V' bottom shape has a similar beneficial effect, but the board will tend to bounce from one flat surface (chine) to the other.

The bottom area further aft is where the board's speed is derived from, and the elliptical roll or 'V' tends to fade, though not completely, since at high speed this area will be the first point of contact with the water.

To gain manoeuvrability, a 'V' is used in the tail area which is most pronounced around the fins, and fades as the tail rocker increases. This allows the board to be rocked from rail to rail, as the curve of the planted rail describes the arc of the turn. A 1.25 cm maximum depth 'V' is enough to give really substantial benefits.

The Duck Gybe

A remarkable number of techniques have evolved for the performance of duck gybing. Essentially the initial stages of the carve gybe are followed **(1)**. On approach to sailing downwind the mast hand releases the sail which pivots on the back hand, and from this point a variety of techniques are used.

By initially taking an underhand grip instead of overhand as the sail pivots, the sailor is left with the boom held overhead like a dagger **(2)**. By immediately sweeping the arm across the body towards the opposite shoulder, the rig can be launched on a free flight **(3)** which brings it into the normal sailing position. The sailor then spreads his crossed arms and plucks the rig from the air.

This technique requires a full planing gybe without a stall – otherwise the rig will be blown away before the rider is able to secure it in his grasp. From the moment of front hand release to catching the rig, the board is carved through 90 degrees.

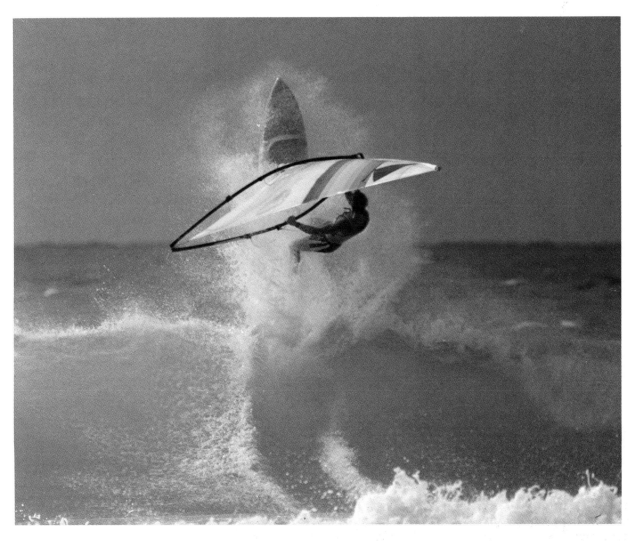

There is a great deal of opportunity for experimentation on bottom profiles. The 'V' and the curved bottom are thoroughly proven standards on which to base your experiments with drop wings, channels, concaves, tunnels, triplanes, bevels etc.

Board Construction

The custom board is a very different story from something produced by a major manufacturer in a matter of minutes (see Manufacturing Techniques). Employing the same materials and techniques as surfboard construction, the builder will spend many exacting hours on a single board.

There are several steps in custom board construction which a professional may specialize in. Shaping, airbrushing, and laminating are completed before fin boxes and textured deck are added. The board is then sanded and polished before the footstraps and mast foot are fitted.

Experience in shaping gives a sound insight into hydrodynamics – subtle changes in shape will affect performance remarkably. Laminating requires the handling of toxic chemicals and teaches the laminator correct balance of chemicals for the climatic conditions present.

To achieve maximum strength-to-weight ratio, the cloth should be

The rider keeps the power on as he jumps from the face of the wave. You can see his track – the wave has already broken on either side.

barely saturated, and the resin should cure as soon as the lamination is complete to gain maximum strength. The work must be completed before the polyester resin cures.

Recent developments in laminating materials have produced superior cloths and resins. Excellent strength and weight is achieved through the use of 3.8 oz S Glass and 6 oz K Glass. These cloths are similar to the conventional sylene and rolan cloths, and easy to work.

Wave Jumping

There are many techniques of jumping employed in order to gain height, length, position in the air and control. Ultimately the techniques evolve into individual styles, but the basics follow the following formula.

Reaching at speed, feet firmly tucked into the straps, aim dead straight into the oncoming wave or 'whitewater'. The nose of the board is lifted as it rides up the ramp **(1)**. Lean towards the tail – otherwise you may be pitched over the nose. If you intend to power the rig during flight **(2)** compensation must be made for the loss of lateral resistance from the fins and rail, for if the normal stance is maintained, the board will drift away downwind. The effect will be reduced if the sail is luffed during flight, but height, length and control are decreased.

To gain power and control through the jump, swing hips and upper body to leeward in over the board and towards the rig at the last moment before take-off.

Initially it may be difficult to convince your body to obey these instructions, but relax and the results will be promising. Keep sheeting in and leaning back. The board will respond to your foot and leg movements easily in the air. Press down on the toes of your back foot in order to lift the windward rail and expose the bottom of your board to the wind. The aerodynamic lift created by angling the board can significantly increase airtime.

During flight, endeavour to push the nose downwind by extending the front leg and powering the rig. The board will thus be pointing more directly on a downwind course when you land. Aim to land tail first **(3)**, on the windward rail. Knees and ankles must flex a little to absorb the impact on landing.

Visualize the steps for a perfect jump in your mind before making the attempt. It is best to have worked them out ashore before you take to your board.

A wave sailing board will be laminated with varying thicknesses. The bottom should have two layers of 6 oz which overlap the rail to give a strong four-layer lamination where it meets the two 6 oz layers on the deck. There should be a third overlay on the deck area from the mast foot to the tail of the board, and additional patches (four layers in all) in the footstrap positions; where the wishbone strikes the deck in the event of a wipe-out; and around the mast foot.

Polyester resin is most often used because of its easily controlled curing time. Standard blanks of polyurethane foam (Clark Foam) are suited to this resin, while slower-curing epoxy resin can only be used on polystyrene foam – the advantage of epoxy resin is that it is more flexible and thus less likely to shatter on impact.

If you wish to build your own board it will take several attempts before you get to a halfway decent standard. For the patient, diligent craftsman there is the chance to bag material is laminated to the deck and after curing is ripped off. This provides an excellent deck texture.

Another method is to sift foam dust (excess from shaping) on to the resin. This gives a good grip but may require light sanding to prevent abrasion.

Reading Waves

Outstanding performers have developed the ability to read waves from years of surfing experience. By predicting how a wave will break, a wave sailor is able to manoeuvre in the critical section of the wave – the part which is breaking and peeling – by using subtle body movements. Athletic prowess is desirable, but it plays a secondary role to knowing what's going on – learning to read waves takes longer than learning the techniques for riding them.

Waves break near the shore when the water depth is less than 1.3 times the wave height from trough to crest. Thus a 3 m wave will begin breaking in 4 m of water, but if the water then deepens, the crumbling lip will stop breaking and re-form. If the depth decreases rapidly, instead of crumbling, the crest will rise and pitch out a foaming 'tube', and then break with considerable violence.

There are basically two different kinds of ocean waves. Long walls of evenly spaced ground swells travel from distant storms, while 'chop' is created by local winds. Ground swells are most suited to wave riding, becoming compacted into rising crests and steepening faces as the 'set' approaches the shore.

Below: 'Reading' waves is the most important part of coping with them, and is the most difficult to learn.

produce a board approaching professional standards within a year or two, but it is not easy, and you must seek professional advice.

Mast Location

Boards 2.75 or 3 metres long usually have the mast foot 1.8 m from the tail. 2.1 m and 2.5 m boards have them at 1.65 m and 1.8 m.

Footstraps

The straps should allow the feet to be slid in and out easily. A firm webbing makes the strap stand up rather than collapse on the deck. To prevent friction burns and blisters, wrap around 3 or 4 mm neoprene.

Be sure the footstraps are spaced to allow a comfortable stance. Average stances vary from 50 to 60 cm. Always position them for high wind sailing, since this is when they are really needed.

Textured Decks

Control of the board is greatly enhanced by a good firm grip. Nylon

Wave Sailing Technique

Physical and mental conditioning are vitally important to the wave-sailor. If a jog around the block inspires palpitations, then it is not a good idea to head out into overhead surf! You will find that sailing in waves makes far greater demands on you than flat water in every respect.

The best preparation is to slip on a pair of swim fins (wetsuit if necessary) and play in the waves where you intend to sail. Familiarity breeds confidence, and is achieved much more economically than tumbling around with the board and rig. Try body surfing, and check your swimming, which must be more than adequate for the conditions.

Before You Go

1. Are you and your rig right for the conditions?
2. Is the rig firmly attached and leashed to the board?
3. Where will you blow to in the event of equipment failure?
4. Are you familiar with the break (waves) at this spot? If not, have you watched carefully, and asked the locals?
5. Are there shallow spots where you may break out a fin box?
6. Can you stand on the bottom, or might you cut your feet?
7. Is the surf rising/falling?

Beach Start

It may not be your burning desire to prove your brilliance to an audience on shore, but falling around amongst fragments of broken mast in the shorebreak rarely gives joy to the unfortunate sailor.

The first priority is a feasible launching site. If rideable waves are breaking outside, then the shoreline is unlikely to be calm. A plunging overhead shorebreak is difficult, and gets impossible in stronger winds.

Look for a gentle slope on the shore. This is likely to be best protected. Watch and get a feel for the rhythm of the shore break and judge approaching waves. When you're confident you've found the right place, carry the board down to the water.

Grab the mast with your windward hand just below the wishbone, and the front windward footstrap with your other hand. Raise the nose of the board by pulling up with the mast hand, while keeping

Critical descent of a wave demands perfect timing plus the ability to gybe out of trouble.

the board level with the back hand. If your board is nose heavy and awkward to transport like this, simply cant the mast across in front of your forehead, and support the rig and nose of the board with your head pushing up on the sail window.

In this manner even the biggest wave boards can be carried to the water's edge, ready to beach start into the surf.

Wind Direction

The most suitable wind direction for wave sailing is sideshore, with a tolerance of 45 degrees either side. It's best of all if the wind is blowing parallel to the shore, since waves can be caught both left and right,

and you get a good speed going out through the whitewater.

When the wind blows onshore, cutting through whitewater at speed is less easy. On a beam reach the waves will strike the windward rail of the board from nose to tail, and heading up into the oncoming whitewater and lifting the windward rail will help guide the board cleanly up and over the whitewater. Otherwise the board is liable to be washed shoreward and to leeward, causing the rig to loose power and come down on top of the sailor. This is where water starts come in useful – just wait for the whitewater to pass over your head.

Riding or surfing waves in more onshore winds causes a substantial reduction in the apparent wind, as the board and the wind begin travelling in much the same direction. Thus the board is heavily relied on for directional control, and since little drive is coming from the rig, it will tend to feel mushy and unresponsive.

When the wind veers offshore, it is liable to be gusty. Returning to the shore will require sailing partially upwind with the waves being used to assist progress. Sailing out through whitewater is made easy, since the waves can be approached directly with optimum speed on a board reach, though the lee side of the wave is liable to harbour turbulent conditions. Obviously an offshore wind will to some extent flatten the waves.

If you sail out through the waves on a close reach, remember to lift the leeward rail (which will hit the wave first) to direct the board up and over, rather than into the wave. The board will tend to be thrust shoreward and into the wind, and therefore the power on the rig is liable to increase dramatically, launching an unprepared rider into his sail. To counter this, depress the windward rail and lean back against the rig as the whitewater pushes the board shorewards.

Getting Out

The techniques for getting out through the waves are similar, irrespective of wind direction.

Hitting an oncoming wall of whitewater tilts the sailor forward. To counter this and help lift the nose, transfer your weight to the back foot and use your knees to absorb the rise in the board. The board will be slowed, but pumping the rig will bring it back to a plane much more swiftly.

Approaching the last breaking wave requires anticipation of its peeling action. The whitewater is most turbulent as the wave initially breaks, while beside it the unbroken wave offers the highest and steepest sections to jump. At first it is wise to stay away from this critical section, since a few tenths of a second will make all the difference between a tail-first and a nose-first landing – the latter is highly undesirable and will be induced by the wave breaking over the nose as you begin to take off. At this point, baling out and throwing the rig and board clean away is the safest course of action.

Riding a short board, the sailor is dealing with a twitchy, sensitive tool. Weight placement becomes critical. To gain good speed in marginal planing conditions, pumping helps but is wasted unless board trim is good. Keeping the board level from rail to rail, with weight forward so as to bring the nose about 15 cm clear of the surface, helps speed greatly.

Getting upwind without a daggerboard is achieved in one of two ways. In heavy airs, getting on the plane and just carrying it as close to the wind as possible works well, but in lighter winds when planing is hard to sustain on a close reach, a second technique is required. Push the windward rail deep in the water and by moving forward extend the waterline length of the board to its maximum – the board then behaves like a long daggerboard.

Speed Sailing with Jaap van der Rest

Dutch born Jaap van der Rest has made a speciality of speed sailing, and in particular the World Speed Sailing Record.

In 1980 he broke this 500 metre record when he sailed a windsurfer special at an average of 24.45 knots. He then went on to push the record to 25.1 knots in 1981, before this record was obliterated by the Frenchman Pascal Maka at Weymouth in 1982, whose 27.82 knot run broke the 50 kph barrier.

Jaap started windsurfing when he was fourteen, and raced for three or four years until he got fed up with the rules and the ultra-serious attitude of the competitors. He then joined the Ten Cate team with their special speed boards designed by Californian Gary Seaman, sailing with them for two years until he first broke the record.

What does it take to sail through a course that fast? As a discipline it bears very little relation to triangle racing, wave riding, freestyle, or any of the other aspects of specialized windsurfing.

It revolves solely around the sailor who can propel his windsurfer fastest through a 500 metre course with his run officially timed. There are major 'speed trials' in the UK (Portland Harbour near Weymouth is the original), France, Germany, Holland and Hawaii, where precise timing is available. The boards that attend them are specially built for the purpose.

Most speed trials are set up so that the boards can reach through the course, sailing as broad a reach as possible. Ideal conditions are a flat sea with a lot of wind, and half the competitor's skill lies in keeping going until he gets the right run.

During 1981 Jaap took part in the three major World Speed Trials; and broke his own record. By following his explanation of what took place at them one can get some idea about what happened in the world of speed boards, where there was a single very radical development. The three speed trials took place in Weymouth, Brest and Veere, and each one has its own very different character.

Weymouth

The speed trials in Weymouth are the oldest ones of all, and their character is typically English.

Until a few years ago only enthusiastic eccentrics took part, arriving at the start in outrageous looking vessels – the event is open to any sailing craft, and not only windsurfers.

Many of these odd craft never really worked. Their masts bent, the hull (or hulls) broke in half, and sometimes the owner would spend the whole week tinkering on the beach without putting to sea at all.

In 1981 the situation at the Weymouth trials had changed from previous years. Windsurfers had totally taken over the 10 Square Metre category, squeezing out all the other sailing craft, and the World Record holder *Crossbow* decided not to participate. She had recorded 36 knots, and with 180 square metres of sail did not want to take the risk of colliding with one of the smaller craft.

There were a variety of interesting boards present. A stepped board with a pintail stern seemed a good idea, since it would plane on the front of the step and the last 40 centimetres of the board alone; there was the Carlsberg Special, but that never seemed to go afloat; there was the previous record holder Clive Colenso, experimenting with an aluminium honeycomb construction; and last but not least

Left: Van Der Rest at speed on the board he used in Weymouth and Brest, before he became convinced that Jürgen Honsheid had found the answer to going faster by sailing a simple surfboard.

Right: The surfboard style windsurfer had been pioneered by Honsheid earlier that year (1981) in Hawaii for sailing and jumping in waves. This 1982 Robbie Naish board has all the high speed characteristics.

there were the Gary Seaman designed Ten Cate boards for Erika and Jaap Keller, Jan Marc Schreur, and myself.

Things started well when I put in the fastest speed on the first day of 22.9 knots. I expected to win the week with ease.

A few days passed quietly, and then I had a rude awakening. The West German/Hawaiian maestro Jürgen Honsheid had turned up with a stock Tiki surfboard, the only board to have less volume and wetted surface area than my own. He stuck a windsurfer rig up near the bow, and then proceeded to sail up and down the course as if he was out in Force 4 – in fact it was blowing near Force 9!

I broke my skeg, another sailor broke his ribs, and Jürgen broke my record with a run of 24.75 knots – but it wasn't fast enough to beat my record by the required 2 per cent (to allow for timekeeping inaccuracy) so I was allowed to keep it!

Brest

Four days were left to prepare for the Speed Cup in Brest on the north-west corner of France. I was worried about Jürgen, but I expected to beat him when I had repaired my skeg.

The Brest week is set up very differently from Weymouth. Four sponsors were present in great style, with prizes, press, entertainment every night, and a gigantic wall of televisions to tell the spectators what was happening.

They laid a big circular course just like the one on Portland Harbour, but the trouble was that it was at least four kilometres offshore.

The spectators were stuck with televisions rather than seeing the real thing; it took a long time to sail out to the course; the waves were enormous whenever the wind started to blow; and there was absolutely no control on the starting procedure. As a result, whenever

Above: Another pintail surfboard/ windsurfer seen in Hawaii in 1982. Note how the stern of the board tapers along both rails to give the minimum wetted area.

Below: The 'conventional' Weymouth speedcraft have been gradually pushed out by the windsurfers, even though entries have been limited to 15 boards.

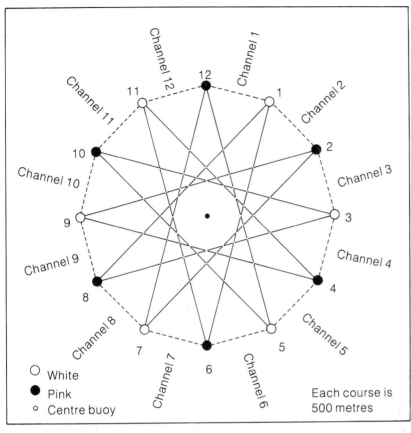

Channel 1
Channel 2
Channel 3
Channel 4
Channel 5
Channel 6
Channel 7
Channel 8
Channel 9
Channel 10
Channel 11
Channel 12

○ White
● Pink
∘ Centre buoy

Each course is 500 metres

Left: The Portland Harbour course is laid out by the RYA each October hopefully to coincide with the equinoctial gales. They lay a circle of buoys, with one buoy in the centre, so that entrants have a choice of 12 Channels with a direct distance of 500 metres – they choose the Channel that best suits their angle of attack.

When it blows very hard, this course becomes too rough for the windsurfers to sail fast through the waves, and the RYA lays on an alternative single Channel 'inshore course' which runs parallel to the beach in shallow water. This is where the boards tend to achieve their best speeds, though they are frequently limited by the angle of the wind to the course.

Below: Jürgen Honsheid at Weymouth in 1981, and about to give Jaap van der Rest a very nasty shock. His board is so small you can barely see it amid the spray. Jürgen learnt his techniques for this type of sailing in Hawaii.

there was a good gust, the course changed into a kind of Champs Elysées during the rush hour.

The last straw was the large number of offshore trimarans and catamarans which the organizers had encouraged to take part in the event. I was run down by one, and then they deliberately sabotaged the inshore course which was used on the one day when it blew hard. They sailed across it, and then lay idle in the middle of it. It goes without saying that these incidents did not improve the atmosphere.

However the presence of the RYA observer, Sir Reginald Bennett, did benefit the atmosphere. Sir Reginald is very aristocratic, and very popular with the sailors. His speeches are unusual in being excellent, and he was the only person to attack the French publicly for giving such precedence to these large boats.

Erika Keller found time to become 'la plus vite femme du monde' with a speed of 20.3 knots. She won 12,500 francs for her trouble, while I found that Jürgen was still going faster than me – the smaller wetted surface area of his board was proving decisive.

Veere

I had two weeks to design and build a new board for the Pall Mall Speed Trials in Veere.

First I modified an ordinary surfboard into a windsurfer and started to practice on it. With the information from this I then built a new board in the remaining four days.

The finish of the board left much to be desired, and then there was no wind for my planned test days. So, there I was at the Veere Speed Trials with a board I had never sailed before, and which might

Stephan Peyron during Weymouth Speed Week 1981. Weymouth is the oldest speed trial, but still remains highly rated owing to the relatively flat water of Portland Harbour in a gale.

need a lot of alterations. Yet I had no other choice, for I knew that Honsheid would beat me if I sailed my old board.

The Pall Mall Speed Trials are unique. The timing is by video cameras and is accurate within hundredths of a second; the course is so near to the shore that the public can easily follow the event; and the safety boat back-up for competitors is excellent.

The week started with very light winds. On the third day I put in quite a fast time – and then on my last run on Friday 13th November I broke the record with a new speed of 25.2 knots.

Above: Jaap's original record-breaking board which he used up until the 1981 Pall Mall Speed Trials. Designed by Gary Seaman it had some 'shape' and buoyancy, while the new style of surfboard pioneered by Jürgen Honsheid (right) at Weymouth opted for the utmost simplicity.

By the speed trials of Autumn 1982, every competitor was relying on a sinker surfboard and a great deal of wind. At Brest, Philip Pudenz set a new record of 26.5 knots, but it was short-lived, for Pascal Maka ran at 27.82 knots at Weymouth two weeks later. Six other sailors exceeded 26 knots, all of whom sailed very similar surfboards, while Jaap van der Rest could only increase his speed to 25.2 knots.

The design of these surfboards is certainly important, but it is mainly the technique of the sailors that seems to govern their speed. Most of those who exceeded 26 knots are noted strong wind specialists, with a great deal of Hawaiian experience behind them – Fraser Black, Jürgen Honsheid, Philip Pudenz and Baron Arnaud de Rosnay are the best-known names.

Freestyle with Ken Winner

Freestyle windsurfing has developed over the past decade from an elaborate excuse to fall into the water to a combination of gymnastics and ballet. It includes pirouettes and flips, jumps and splits. There are now competitions world wide with hundreds of freestylists entered. We have judges, rules, compulsory tricks, and fixed routines. It's even grown to the point that there are freestyle specialists – sailors who do only freestyle. None of this complexity, however, can diminish the primary appeal of freestyle – it's still a heck of a good excuse to fall into the water.

1976 was the year my own interest in freestyle surfaced. I was twenty one and had little better to do than spend my hours away from school splashing about in the water attempting Head Dips and Water Starts. English literature and calculus had little chance against the water's lure on a warm, breezy spring day. It's ironic that my hours on the water have given me a better vocation than my time in the classroom ever could.

'76 was also the year of the Railride. Railriding had been done before but Robbie Naish, then only 12 years old, brought a better technique to North America and then the world. The Railride became the most appealing trick around that year, the fanciest thing you could do on a board, and it focused considerable attention on freestyle windsurfing. Doing freestyle, riding the rail, was how you showed the crowd at the beach that you weren't just another boardsailor. Boys became men through the simple act of putting a sailboard on edge.

The following year freestyle became an event at the Windsurfer World Championships in Sardinia, Italy. With this new distinction came controversy. Who should the judges be? Should there be a large penalty for falls? Should spectacu-

Above: American born Ken Winner, one of the early World Freestyle Champions, a winner of the Pan Am Cup, and a prototype designer for Dufour.

lar tricks or graceful tricks be encouraged? Never mind what the judges say, who really won? Each year at major freestyle competitions these questions are asked, and answered. The answers change as the sport evolves, as the competitors become more skilled and the judges more perceptive, but the questions remain the same. It is the presence of these questions, these controversies, that show freestyle's vitality, its appeal to a broad range of people.

That range of people includes the competitors, of course, but more importantly, it includes the many sailors who do freestyle for neither glory, nor money, but rather for fun: the fun of being in the open air, feeling the wind in hand and the water under foot, the pleasure of seeing the world upside-down through a Head Dip, or the giddy sensation of twirling in a Pirouette.

It also includes people who enjoy the challenge of a new trick, the satisfaction of learning it well, and who in turn want to teach it to a friend. And it includes those who just need a good excuse to fall into the water.

Right: British Freestyle Champion Dee Caldwell demonstrates the Everole as part of his routine. Dee mastered the art of freestyle by training in the Bahamas during the winter months.

Somersaulting through the wishbone looks good if you can manage to fit between the wishbone and the sail, and land back on the board while keeping sailing. However it's difficult, and most sailors use it as the 'dismount' part of their routine, when they are happy to finish up in the water with a big splash.

The Background
Freestyle has developed from 'hot dogging' which was an undisciplined way of having fun on a board.

The Americans were first to develop it into a proper routine, and it was the American born Windsurfer class that began to run competitions similar to the freestyle events famil-iar to skaters.

That was the 1970's, and since that time routines have got slicker, and more and more polished. The time when a railride was greeted by exclamations is long gone, and now it's the people who can't do it who stand out like a sore thumb – and freestyle competitions are held during most weekend regattas.

Freestyle and Its Uses

There are not many top regatta sailors who can't at least manage the basics of freestyle. The ability to know the limits of a board's manoeuvrability are vital when you're juggling for position on a windy start line, or rounding a mark with a mass of other boards when there will inevitably be collisions.

For instance, at the start you frequently need to sail backwards away from the line; if you fall off, it's a lot quicker to be able to recover with a water start; and when you infringe the rules, it's time for a high speed 720 degree turn, which only a freestylist knows how to do best – by mastering a freestyle routine, you can get out of all these unexpected messes.

Freestyle Routine

The normal pattern in a regatta is for each contestant to be allotted three minutes in which to perform his or her routine. The signal for starting is when the contestant drops one arm, and then the judges loud-hail him when the time is up, with a 30 second warning and a 15 second countdown.

Freestyle Judging

The contestant needs to perform a wide variety of tricks with a smooth and stylish transition from one to the next.

In a big international competition, there will be four judges who will evaluate the performance in each of the following categories:
1. Number of tricks performed.
2. Technical difficulty of tricks performed.
3. The originality of the routine.
4. Style in the execution of the tricks.
5. Style in the execution of the routine as a whole.

Each category is marked out of 20, and the marks of the four judges are averaged out. When there are a great many competitors,

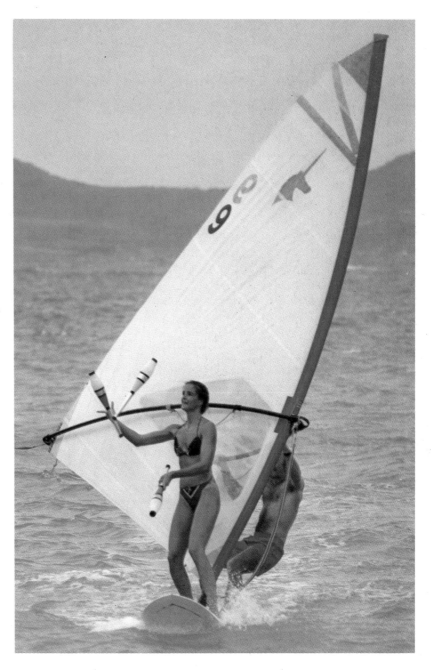

there will be preliminary rounds, quarter and semi finals, and finals.

In smaller local events it is only necessary to have two or three judges, and you can work out a simpler marking system – competitors don't often argue with the judges. If the standard is low, you can make do with shorter routines of two minutes or less.

It's not in the normal tricks repertory, but there are occasional competitions for two-up freestyle, and if you can juggle, why not? The normal combination for this kind of thing is a father and his very small son, or a boy and his girlfriend, but it's seldom taken very seriously. However, it can bring some light relief to a regatta.

Preparation and Basics

The ideal freestyle board should be a flatboard with wide deep rails, which is stable and easy to sail, but at the same time responsive and quick to manoeuvre.

Typical favourites are the Windsurfer Regatta and Mistral Competition. They frequently have a cutdown skeg to help the board turn really fast – sailing in a straight line is not a requisite of a good freestyle routine!

Vital Points

A freestyle board needs as careful preparation as a board for regatta racing or wave jumping.

Non-slip. There is no way you should slip on that board. If there is any chance of doing so, use board wax, and not just on the deck. When you're rail riding you'll need to use the sides and bottom, so wax those as well.

Mast foot. Under no circumstances should it come out, and you will be putting constant pressure on it to see you and your board through a trick – you spend a lot of time levering the mast against the deck of the board in order to keep it up on the rail. Screw it up really tight, or if it's a T-piece, tape it up and hammer it in.

Daggerboard. When you're on the rail you'll want to step on and off it, so wax it as well. Make sure it's not a sloppy fit which will slide out when you flip up the board. On the other hand you don't want it jammed in rock solid – it's handy to pull it halfway so that you can use it as a step on the deck side of the board when you're going on to the rail.

Sails

You should also consider which sail to use. When you're developing and learning tricks it's best to have a light wind, but when you do your award winning routine you need plenty of power in the sail to support those body dips and somer-saults. If the sail is too small or too flat you'll be dropping into the water in the middle of every trick, so make sure it's easily handled and the right size – the ideal is a high clew battenless sail with a steady Force 3 wind over a pancake flat sea.

Clothing

The fewer clothes you wear, the more agile you are – but that's only OK if the water is warm and you're experienced enough not to get covered in bruises and bashes.

When you start, you'll find that your shins and feet are particularly susceptible – you'd do best to wear a long john with reinforced shin pads, and some windsurfing shoes that grip like limpets.

Basic Tricks

All freestylists should learn to master the basic tricks before they move on to the more rarefied variations and their own inventions – there's always someone who comes up with something new and startling just once or twice a year!

These are the basic tricks which were worked out by the Windsurfer class all those years ago:

Quick tack
Like it says.
Quick Gybe
Likewise.
Power Gybe
Pushing the board through the eye of the wind by forcing the rig against the wind to turn the board. Much used in racing and strong wind sailing.
Head Dip
Sticking your head in the water while sailing – you can do it either backwards or forwards. It's good exercise for your back.
Body Dip
Lowering your body in the water while still sailing – and then letting the rig lift you out again.
Water Start
Not that dissimilar to the above. Starting sailing when you're lying in the water is useful when you have an inadvertent fall during your freestyle routine. Also much used by those sailing 'sinkers'.
Stern First
Sailing along with your stern leading the way.
Inside the Wishbone
Sailing along with your body stuck up between the wishbone and the sail. You can do it on the windward or the leeward side.
Leeward Side Sailing
Standing there, pushing the rig from the leeward side while you're sailing along.
Back to the Sail
Doing the above with your back to the sail, and looking very cool.
Sitting
Like it says.
Lying
Ditto, and you can go so far as to try the splits.
Sail 360
Turning the rig through 360 degrees while the board keeps sailing in a straight line. Alternatively you can try a board 360 which will come in useful when you have to do all those penalty 720's on the race course.
Railride
Flip the board up on its side and stand on the rail. There are many variations: you can go backwards; forwards; inside the wishbone; etc.
Tail Sink
Sinking the back end, which is useful for nice slow gybes.
Dismount
Any way you want to finish your routine, so long as it is dramatic/graceful. Climb to the top of the mast, somersault through the wishbone, or simply catapult into mid air. It's important to get the timing right, and if it's good you'll raise a cheer from the spectators.

Flying high with a tail-sink as the culmination of a freestyle routine. Finishing off with a dramatic trick is all part of impressing the judges.

Basic Railride

Sail along on a reach. To flip the
board up, push down on the
leeward rail with your back foot,
while pulling up the windward rail

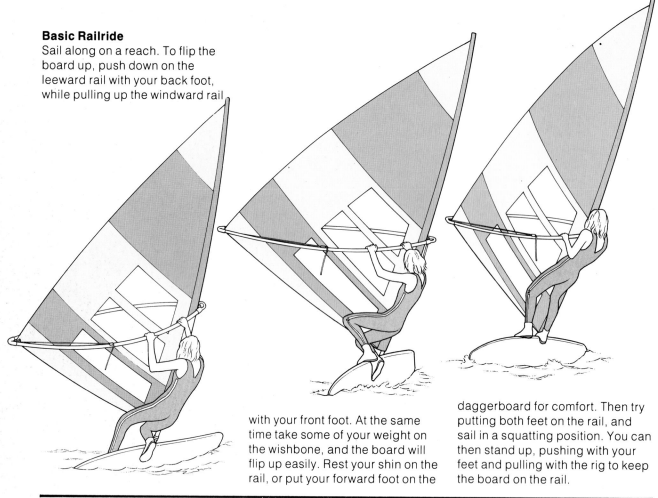

with your front foot. At the same
time take some of your weight on
the wishbone, and the board will
flip up easily. Rest your shin on the
rail, or put your forward foot on the

daggerboard for comfort. Then try
putting both feet on the rail, and
sail in a squatting position. You can
then stand up, pushing with your
feet and pulling with the rig to keep
the board on the rail.

First Attempts

You should learn trick by trick.
Pick out the one you want to do,
and then work at it until you've got
it right, rather than giving up and
going on to the next one.

If you can, rehearse the trick on
dry land. You'll find that you can
run through almost the whole
routine, including railrides.

When you come to try the trick
on the water, make sure it's flat,
shallow, with the wind around
Force 2. Ideally the water should be
warm as well.

Working out a Routine

Master your individual tricks until
you've got each one right – in light
winds, medium winds, and strong
winds.

You can then string them together into a routine, where one

trick should lead on gracefully to
the next.

There is no way you can do this
by intuition alone. Sure, you have
to know enough to improvize and
grab opportunities if something
goes wrong or conditions change,
but your basic routine for those
three minutes should have been
worked out to perfection by you
months before.

Favourites

All the tricks are variations on a
theme of good board control. These
are favourites for a good freestyle
routine.

Railride

This is the one you have to be able
to do. When you get really good,
you can do it backwards, forwards,
inside the wishbone, to windward

or to leeward of the rig, and on
(what was) the windward or leeward rail of the board. You can also
rock 'n' roll it as you go along.

The basic railride is a matter of
balance, and preventing the board
from heading up into the wind,
which it will always be inclined to
do. You should be sure to master
the simple art of flipping up the
windward rail and sailing along,
before you move on to any of the
more ornate variations on this
theme. If you find you're slipping
on the board, you can rough up the
surface with a rasp.

Right: The fine art of balancing on
the rail is the basis of a freestyle
routine. Once you have mastered it
you can improvize a succession of
different tricks, illustrated on the
following pages.

as the board flips up put both feet on the rail (**2**) and stand up (**3**). A relatively flat board such as the Windsurfer will sail as well backwards as forwards when it's up on the rail like this. More variations follow.

Railride Backwards
Sail the board backwards, travelling skeg first. Push down on the lee rail with your back foot while lifting the windward rail with your front foot (**1**). At the same time take your weight on the wishbone, and

Railride Variations
A world class freestyle sailor can sail on the rail rather better than most of us can sail with the board flat on the water, but it just takes hours of practice.

Railriding heading backwards is a little more difficult than the basic technique, and railriding on the leeward rail is a little more difficult still.

An interesting variation on the lee side railride is the 'Everoll' developed by American Gary Eversole, who also invented the 'Rock 'n' Roll' (on boards). The Everoll is a railride taken just a little too far. You sail clew first to the wind, and then flip up the leeward side of the board, letting it rest against the mast when it comes up, so that you can stand on the daggerboard on the bottom of the windsurfer. Once you're set up like this you can control the angle of the board by

sheeting in and out. Obviously it is important that the daggerboard is fixed fairly firmly in place.

Recovery
If you mess it up and fall in, it is imperative that you can recover as neatly and swiftly as possible. A water start is the smartest way to start up again.

The easiest way to learn the basics of a water start is to let yourself fall back into the water on purpose. Sail along on a reach, and then let out your sheet hand so that you fall back with the rig on top of you.

So long as you lift the rig clear of the water, and keep the board beam on to the wind, you will find that once you sheet back in, the rig will lift you out and back on your feet.

If the wind is light it's tricky, and you may need to give it a helping hand. Bend your knees to get your weight inboard, and if that's no good shift your hands down from the wishbone to the base of the rig. The mast hand can hold the rig a couple of feet above the deck, while the sheet hand grabs the foot of the sail about one-third of the way back. This way the rig should have enough leverage to lift you right out again. Remember that the board will want to head up into the wind. Obviously it's easier if you're a lightweight.

Right: Dee Caldwell sitting on the rail and looking very wet. His next move will be to tuck his feet up so he can stand on the rail.

Reverse Railride
Sail along on a reach and start to push down the windward rail (**1**). At the same time help to lift the leeward rail with your other foot, while taking your weight on the wishbone (**2**). As the board flips up, stand on the rail (**3**). You can then move one foot forward of the mast for your next trick (**4**).

This is a lot trickier than a conventional railride, since you need a lot more balance to keep the board up on the rail. You must play the pressure of the mast against the side of the board very carefully, or it will flip back down again. This is when it is particularly important to have the mast foot jammed solidly into position – there must be no way that it can come unstuck during your routine.

Rock 'n' Roll

Sail along on the rail, either forward or backwards. With your feet spread fairly well apart, you can then rock the board, dipping the nose and the stern alternatively. It is important not to slip, and to try and do this trick gracefully with an easy motion. A lot of sailors do it very jerkily and in a hurry, and it just looks a mess.

This trick was first seen at the Windsurfer World Championship in Sardinia in 1977, and has been part of the repertoire ever since.

Water Start Practice

You can practice the basics of the water start on the beach and in shallow water.

The main point to remember is that you must keep the board beam on the wind, with the rig on its windward side. The problem then is likely to be the board sliding around as you try to get back on your feet. It may try heading up or bearing away at inopportune moments, and you have to control this by pushing your feet against the windward rail of the board, keeping it at right angles to the wind.

If you have a normal sized daggerboard and reasonably well balanced skeg, the board should not

Left: Power and precision as a sailor pirouettes during his freestyle routine. Tricks should always be graceful. To win you should be as impressive and as fluid as an ice skating champion.

slide around too much. The problems are likely to be far more severe when you're trying to water start a sinker with a single skeg and minimum lateral resistance – this strong wind technique is covered on page 116.

Whatever you do, try not to drop the rig right down flat on the surface of the water. If you do so, trying to push up the sail to catch the wind will prove very difficult for all but experts.

Towing

If it's windy enough, and the board is travelling fast, you can come near to walking on water.

Sail along on a broad reach, and then simply step backwards off the board on to the water. You won't be able to run fast enough to keep up with it, but you can allow your body to be towed like an old bundle for a few seconds. When the rig starts collapsing or the board starts bearing off, it's time to pull in with

your arms and get back on the board pretty smartly.

This trick would look good as a lead-up to a somersault through the wishbone, followed by a flare gybe to get you going back in the opposite direction.

Finally, whatever you do, don't get carried away during your routine with a sequence of tricks on one tack that ends up two miles from the judges. They don't appreciate having to use binoculars!

Railride Inside the Wishbone

This is a lot more difficult than it looks, and needs a lot of practice if you're not going to end up falling in. It's also a difficult trick to recover from gracefully if you do fall in, so don't put it in your routine until you know you're not going to mess it up.

Sail along on a regular railride – it doesn't matter whether it's nose or stern first. Be sure to keep a fairly broad reach, and when you're comfortable (**1**), tuck your head up

inside the wishbone, supporting it with the back of your neck (**2**). You can then wriggle your body through, while keeping a firm grip on the wishbone with your hands and arms (**3**). Once you're up

inside the wishbone, you have to be very careful not to let the board round up head to wind. Remember that your movement is limited, so it's difficult to respond quickly to any gusts. It's best if you move

your forward hand to the mast (**4**), which will at least give you a little more leverage and response from the rig. This should always be raked well forward.

A trick like this should flow on as a continuous part of a railride, and can be combined with other specialities such as rock 'n' roll and gybing on the rail, before reverting to some tricks, such as helicopters and hirondelles, which are accomplished when the board is flat on the water. If you want to do these tricks in the right sequence, you must learn from watching the top sailors.

Railride Clew-first

You can sail with the rig turned 180 degrees the wrong way, so that the clew is pointing into the wind. It's not as efficient as sailing with the rig the right way round, but it does work.

To sail clew-first, gybe the board round to the opposite reach, but keep the sail on its original side. Don't let the board come round any closer than a broad reach or the wind will hit the sail on

Other Tricks

A good basic trick to get the hang of is sailing with your back to the leeward side of the sail. It looks easy and it looks cool.

You start off by building up speed on a close reach. Then, let your sheet hand go and grab the mast a couple of feet down from the wishbone. At the same time let go with your mast hand, and step round the front of the mast so that you're on the lee side of the sail. You can then change the hand holding the mast, and rake the rig forward as you push back with the other arm outstretched along the wishbone to sheet in and get sailing.

You must remember to keep on a reach. Don't let the board head up or bear away too much, or it will deposit you in the water.

Spin Tack

There's nothing too difficult about this, and it looks pretty good.

Go into a regular tack, but when you step round the front of the mast given a little 180 degree spin on the ball of your foot so that you end up turning through a full 360 degrees.

As you turn, you can grab the rig as necessary if you feel it's going AWOL. So long as your timing is alright, everything will be OK.

Wheelie

A Tail Sink looks pretty clumsy in light winds. The guy just sinks the back of the board, and then clambers back along it to flatten it out.

However if it's windy you can turn it into a full wheelie.

Sail along on a very broad reach as fast as you can – and then jump on to the very back of the board with all your weight. It's the same

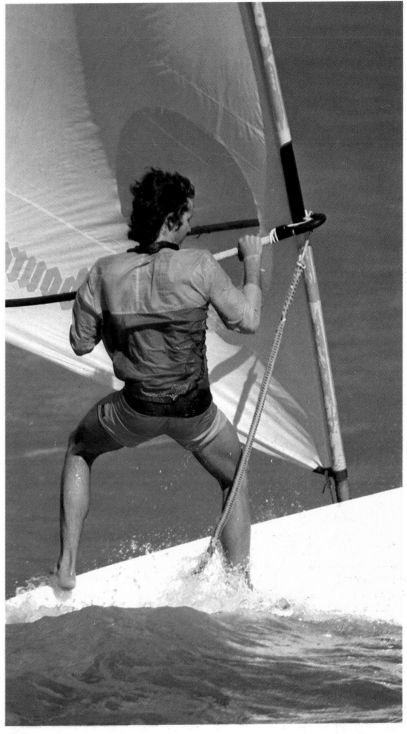

its lee side and take control of you. You can flip the board up on the rail in the conventional manner (**1**), though you will need to keep one foot on the daggerboard to prevent the board flipping right over. You can then gybe the rig (**2/3**) and sail on in the conventional railride position (**4**). Going from tack to tack looks particularly impressive.

process as slowing down for the gybe mark, but hopefully the board will delight the judges as it skips along on its stern before it finally goes down into a regular tail sink.

At this point you can always go into a flare gybe, and head back on the other reach as you prepare for your somersault-on-the-rail routine, which would be a nice way to finish your three minutes. Anyone who invents a new trick is going to score heavily.

Remember, it always pays to finish with some high drama and possible amusement.

Above: When you start to learn to railride it's a lot easier to keep one foot on the daggerboard. Remember to protect your shins for kneeling on the rails. They are very hard on bare skin, and if you're not experienced like Dee Caldwell it's easy to end up with a mass of bruises. Dee is dipping the stern for some rock 'n' roll.

Duck Track Pirouette
This one combines several tricks that can be done while the board is flat on the water – as yet no one has managed to do it on the rail!

Sail along close hauled, but get up a good turn of speed before you go into your tack. Rake the rig aft in the conventional manner. Wait until the nose of the board starts to pass through the eye of the wind – and at this point forget all you know and start learning all over again.

Pause, let go with your mast hand, and then throw the rig well forward with your sheet hand (**1**). Let go of the wishbone altogether, and duck under the foot of the sail

Ladies' Tricks
Ladies can do some tricks which men will find pretty hard to handle, mainly because of the different way in which we are put together.

A windsurfer is an ideal platform for the splits, but you should know how to do it on dry land before giving it a go on the sea.

As with most tricks, it's easiest to start on a reach – it gives you plenty of power and enough latitude for recovery if things go wrong.

Head up on to a close reach, and begin to slide your front foot forward, followed by your back foot. If the wishbone is high you may have to drop your hands on to the mast and the foot of the sail.

The board will start to head up into the wind, particularly if it is blowing hard, so you need to get back on to your feet fairly rapidly.

Somersault
The somersault through the wishbone is a good way to finish off your routine, though if you land up on your feet still sailing, you have to think of another dismount in double quick time.

You really need a minimum of Force 3 to make it worthwhile, and the windier it is, the more spectacular the trick will be.

The theory is simple. You sail on a close reach, and when you're ready, sheet out a little to give you enough room to kick up and go through the wishbone feet first. You've got to kick hard and go into

a semi-tuck position to fit through. Also it's got to be the one and only. If you go at it in a half-hearted manner, you'll end up without the impetus to get you through, and the rig will collapse down around your head.

Combinations
Big freestyle events normally include competitions for combinations. These can include two people on one board; two people on two boards sailing along together; even more than two people on one or more boards (trying not to sink them); and two people on a tandem.

None of these are as serious as the regular one-up routine, but the two-up tricks are always good for

(2), ready to grasp the wishbone on the new tack (3) first with your mast hand (4), and then with your sheet hand.

Until you've got the hang of it, it's easier to grab hold of the foot of the sail with one hand as you duck under it – otherwise you're likely to lose the rig altogether.

That was a basic duck tack, but when you're really good you can combine it with the pirouette shown here – rather than simply ducking under the foot of the sail, you pirouette through 360 degrees while you're doing it. Conditions need to be right so that the rig is not blown away from you.

laughs, and are now getting established in the calendar. They tend to attract either a boyfriend/girlfriend duo, or a father and young son. The participants tend to enjoy the first, while the second has the great advantage of one member of the team being unusually light and agile, but with some strength ready to hand if it's needed.

Final Points
1. Prepare the board thoroughly.
2. Master each trick – on the

Right: Back-to-the-sail head dip. The sailor holds on to the rig, but he's facing backwards. It's not as difficult as it looks. However he makes it a little more difficult with a head dip in the water.

Left: A triple team with two boards performs a complex ascent of the rig – it helps when a couple of them are very small, very light, and very agile. This is more exhibitionist freestyle than anything done to a precise competition routine, but it is probably a good way to keep a family amused.

beach, in shallow water, in deep water, in light, medium, and strong winds, and in waves.
3. Work out a routine which is decided upon in advance.
4. Ensure that the tricks flow into one another, and keep you and your board within a relatively small area – you don't want to sail off miles from both judges and spectators.

5. Amuse the audience, and try to look happy.
6. Try to develop your own new variation on a trick.
7. Don't be psyched out by the routines of the competitors who some before you.
8. End your routine with a dramatic flourish – but don't just jump in the water.

Pirouette

During a perfect pirouette the rig hardly moves even though it is unsupported.

To do it this way the board needs to be moving quite fast through the water, and a Force 2 wind is ideal. If the wind is any stronger, there is a danger that the rig will be blown out of your reach by a gust, while if the wind is any lighter, the rig will simply fall over into the water.

It's easiest to do it on a very broad reach, so that when you turn you don't get tangled with the rig and knock it to one side – for this reason you should also keep your arms well in to your body and spin on one foot in a very tight circle.

In the illustration, the sailor has just let go of the rig, and is spinning

anti-clockwise on the ball of her foot (**1**). She turns full circle in a matter of a couple of seconds, ready to grab the wishbone (**2**) and keep sailing (**3**). If you don't get dizzy, you could perform several pirouettes like this in swift succession – they are one of the most graceful manoeuvres in a freestyle routine.

Windsurfing Feats

The flamboyant Baron Arnaud de Rosnay once said that anyone considering windsurfing across the Atlantic had no idea what was involved – it just could not be done.

However, within a year a French airline pilot had done just that, windsurfing the breadth of the Atlantic without leaving his board.

Christian Marty had planned the trip for two years. During that time he took extended leave from Air France to prepare himself. He studied psychology, biology, and climatology; took up cycling, jogging, walking, and hanging from trees (to build up his arm muscles!) and set a couple of first time windsurfing records by sailing from the French Riviera to Corsica, and going around the island of Guadeloupe in 51 hours non-stop.

The trip was budgeted at £100,000, paid for by Marty's three sponsors: the magazine VSD; the radio station Antenne 2; and the board manufacturer Sodim, who provided Marty with his Oversea board, a new 350 cm strong wind design that was selected as being easy to sail and fast in a variety of conditions.

Marty had planned to sail from Dakar in French West Africa to Martinique in the West Indies. He would not leave his board during the crossing, which he estimated at between 28–40 days, and would be accompanied all the way across by a support ship, the 70 foot ketch *Assiduous*, crewed by 12 of his friends. They would bring him his food via the yacht's tender, and at night would prepare him for sleep.

In order to live on his board 24 hours a day for a month, Marty had hit on an ingenious system. He would de-rig his board and hand the whole lot over to the waiting crew in the tender, who would then pass him an inflatable collar with which to encircle his board – the idea was that he could lie down and sleep inside it quite comfortably. He would then rig a short mast with

Above: Christian Marty had three inflatable support boats, which brought him all he needed from *Assiduous*, including his thrice daily meals, and gear for settling down for the night.

a flashlight and radar reflector to make sure he stayed in contact with *Assiduous*. He also planned to fly a small staysail which would pull him along at night, but abandoned this idea as he felt it was cheating.

Marty was equipped with an immense variety of sails, all coloured apple green which was supposed to be easy to spot at sea without being a strain on Marty's eyes (though it turned out that *Assiduous* frequently had difficulty finding him). Just to be safe he took three identical suits of nine sails each, ranging from three to nine square metres.

During the crossing, the predictable Trade Wind was astern, and he devised a sailing system with a harness, an inflatable seat, and a double wishbone, which would allow him to sail sitting down in a comfortable position. Initially he used a high seat, but as the crossing progressed he made it lower and lower until eventually he was sitting on the board.

Departure

Marty left Dakar on November 28th 1981. This was the time of year when he could expect consistently safe conditions in the latitudes he was crossing. The Trades would blow from the North-East at between 15 and 25 knots, giving him a fair wind and a comfortable sea temperature – Doctor Bombard had planned his famous journey in a rubber liferaft along much the same principles.

Marty ran into trouble almost immediately. On the first night he capsized several times while he was sleeping, and was thrown into the water. This was to happen again later on the voyage, but initially he was able to overcome the problem by lowering the safety lamp on the mast until it did not interfere with the balance of the board, and attaching a couple of ship's fenders either side to make it more stable. With a set-up like this he was able to sleep amidst five metre waves when the wind blew up to 32 knots on the third night.

Five days and 150 miles out of Dakar, it was *Assiduous* that ran into trouble, rather than Marty. Her rudder was damaged and the only option was to put back for repairs, before the team could set out once again after a 10 day delay.

The delay forced Marty to change his plans. Most of the crew of *Assiduous* had voluntarily taken time off from their regular jobs, and for everyone time was at a premium. Therefore, he decided to go for the nearest point on the other side of the Atlantic, Cayenne in French Guiana – it was almost 1000 miles closer than Martinique, but still 2400 miles and more than one month distant.

Right: Marty windsurfed eight hours a day, using a secondary wishbone so that he could sit down. As the trip progressed his seat got lower and lower, until he was sitting on the board.

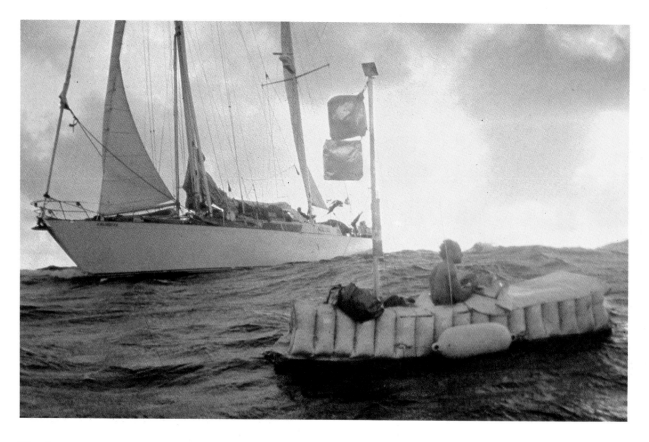

The Crossing

Once underway again, things went well for Marty. He broke the 1000 miles barrier after 17 days, having established a regimen of windsurfing eight hours a day; sleeping six to eight hours a day; and eating three main meals a day.

His food revolved around dried fruit and tea for breakfast; and red meat, vegetables, Gruyère cheese and noodles for both lunch and dinner. On New Year's Eve this diet was radically improved, and *Assiduous* brought him a punch made from the remnants of their rum, plus sausage cocktails, Nantua *quennelles* with American sauce, roast pork with prunes, and apricot pie. At midnight this was followed by champagne and fireworks (distress rockets) let off by the crew!

As on the first attempt it was *Assiduous* that ran into more problems than Marty. First the crew

was seasick, and then the generator broke down. Since they had also managed to flatten the ship's batteries, they were unable to start the engine, and had no light, no radio, no satellite navigation, and nothing to run the galley. For a month this forced them to live in a shambles, with all the cooking for 13 men being done on a small single gas ring in the forecabin. This carried on until eventually one of them hit on the idea of starting the engine with a diving compressor.

Marty carried on regardless, logging 70 and more miles a day on his eight hour shifts 'like someone who has a job'.

His morale stayed consistently high, but was nearly broken by a narrow escape from drowning and increasingly unfavourable currents as he neared the South American coastline.

The near drowning was one of those little incidents in which the

At night Marty would surround his board with an inflatable collar, with a couple of fenders for stability in rough seas.

situation rapidly gets worse. He had capsized whilst sleeping several times before, and it happened once again. He had also lost two sleeping bags this way, and when he saw the third one floating two metres away from him, he tried to get it. He moved away slightly from his board, which was on its side, when it suddenly righted itself. Immediately it began to be carried away by the current faster than Marty could swim – with each stroke, his hand hit the water a foot behind the board and he was unable to catch it. He remembered those moments at the Press Conference a month later. 'I fought for eight minutes. I understood then that I was going to die. This may seem funny but I thought of my children and my wife

Rough and cold weather on the east side of the Atlantic. Until the last days, the wind seldom deserted Marty.

who awaited me at Cayenne. I stopped swimming, and I screamed. By an incredible stroke of good fortune my crew was passing nearby at that moment. They returned me to my board, 300 metres away – that, I will never forget.'

His team had seen nothing. When the board capsized, it was hidden by the swell, and when it came back into view, it had righted itself – they had no reason to assume that anything was amiss.

And if they had not heard him? There is no doubt that Marty would have been lost. Everything designed to help him survive if he became separated from *Assiduous* – VHF/ADF radio, flares, food, water purification system, and compass – was on his board, and he

would never have been seen again.

After this, Marty tethered himself to the board. Progress became slower and slower as they moved through wind and sea conditions that became variable and unpredictable near the Equator. As they got closer to the coast, the powerful Amazonian current set them off course – they were not equipped with the local tide charts.

Eventually, after a week of battling with the Amazon, Marty completed his journey. On 18th January 1982 he surfed the bar at Kourou near Cayenne at 13 knots, and drove up on to the beach.

He had windsurfed the Atlantic, covering 2400 miles of open ocean. He had not left his board for 37 days, 16 hours, and 14 minutes.

Baron Arnaud de Rosnay

Baron Arnaud de Rosnay is a very different animal from the self-effacing Christian Marty.

Born into the wealth of a Mauritian sugar plantation, with French and Russian parents (his father is a painter) de Rosnay is a windsurfing entrepreneur/explorer, always determined to hit the headlines, and always successful in doing so.

First Feats

The Baron has always been an excellent publicist for his feats, which began when he 'landsurfed' the Sahara in 1979.

He had invented what he called a Speed Sail – a sort of windsurfer on wheels looking like a nine foot long skateboard – and wanted to prove its prowess. To do so, he 'landsurfed' 220 miles from the borders of Mauritania to Dakar, with a jeep (carrying a driver, three guides, a photographer and a journalist) in attendance. Sponsorship was provided by the French Channel 2 TV, VSD magazine, and Lacoste clothing.

The Baron's second feat followed close after in the same year. On August 31st he windsurfed across the shortest aquatic distance between Russia and America – the Bering Straits.

In fact he had to go a little further. Sixty-five miles is the direct distance, but that culminates in a 1000 foot high sheer rock face, so he had to cover another 20 miles to find a rather more hospitable landfall.

The conditions were not good. The Straits are only navigable for three summer months every year (the rest of the time it is frozen) and even then the temperature is a mere four degrees Centigrade with strong winds being the norm.

The board chosen by the Baron was a Windsurfer Rocket, dressed up to look like a TC39, which his sponsors, Ten Cate, were marketing. With him he took his passport, $500 in cash, flares, and chocolate – but no sanction from either the US or Russian governments.

Half way over, a Russian destroyer took up station to escort him to their side. It took eight hours to complete the crossing, he lost his gloves, and when he arrived he was so tired and cold that he fell off several times trying to get back to the ship and security, and had to be picked up by a launch.

The fact that he had entered Russia illegally was overlooked. He was entertained to caviar and vodka

Christian Marty dressed for any weather, with a look of indefatigable determination like Lawrence of Arabia.

by the ship's captain, and was then flown to Moscow and on to Paris, where he could begin the planning of his third major feat.

The Pacific
In 1980 the Baron made his most controversial voyage.

He intended windsurfing across the Pacific, from the Marquesas to the islands of Hawaii, retracing the original Polynesian route of discovery. He would be accompanied by a support boat, and like Marty he would never leave his board.

The trip took six months to prepare. He had a specially designed windsurfer which had an inflatable neoprene 'doughnut' round its circumference. He could stand up and windsurf by day, while at night he laid the rig across his board with floats attached to either end of the mast to make the whole contraption into a trimaran. He could then blow up his doughnut, and snuggle down inside it while a parakite pulled him along at 3–5 knots, with the Trade Winds behind. The whole apparatus weighed just over 100 pounds, and was 12 foot long with a 15 foot beam and a 10 inch freeboard.

He had chosen the weather carefully. No storms, and the Trades giving between 17 and 22 knots by day and night. By day he would stand and windsurf, while by night the parakite would continue to power him in the right direction.

All the preparation came to nought when de Rosnay set out on 29th August. His support craft made a bare six knots while he was sailing at 12, and he found that he had to stop and wait for her to catch up every half hour.

The attempt was abandoned, and they had no option but to turn back. However de Rosnay would not give up his plan. Since the authorities refused to allow him to leave without a support craft, he decided to give them the slip, and left once again, alone, and in the middle of the night.

His plans had changed. He would head South rather than North – his main intention seems to have been to cover as much of the open Pacific as possible, with the Tuamotus group of islands being his destination.

Once under way the board and the parakite worked well, but the problems multiplied. He had reckoned on sheltering from the sun behind the sail, but with the effect of salt water he soon had boils on every joint. His lethal-sounding remedy was to windsurf nude and in the full sun for two days, 'to burn off the infection'. From then on he wore a loose fitting Helly Hansen suit, jumping in the water once an hour to cool off.

He was attacked by a couple of sharks, and lived in constant fear of encountering a 10 footer. Nor was his navigation very successful. There was at least a six foot swell, and if he wanted to use his sextant he had to go through the rigmarole of turning his board into a stable trimaran, and then disassembling it. This took a total of 40 minutes, so rather than get his mid-day sight, he put the sextant in its box and sent if off on its way across the ocean. From then on he navigated by compass and dead reckoning – ie estimating his course, and how fast he was travelling.

After sunburn, sharks, and navigation, his fourth great problem was food and water. He had reckoned on being at sea for a week, and had left with one and a half gallons of water, some dates and nuts, and

The great windsurfing pioneer Baron Arnaud de Rosnay is imbued with a delightful air of 19th century eccentricity.

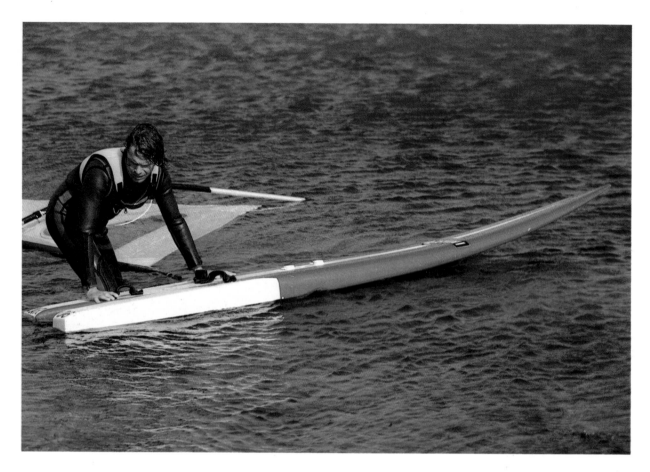

NASA survival tablets – he was later to say, 'they are very terrible to eat – like foie gras surrounded by chocolate'.

He was drinking fresh and sea water in a mix of 2:1 as the NASA nutritionists recommended, but after six days there was very little water left. He had two solar stills, but couldn't use them while he was sailing, and hopefully getting closer to land. A couple of rain showers helped, but after 12 days all the water was gone, and de Rosnay had to abandon sailing, and just lie down and let the parakite pull the board while the stills slowly made him some water.

He was lucky. The following day he found land and he found people. He had reached the Island of Ahe, one of the Tuamotus group, after 750 miles of open water, and had just survived.

However, he was even luckier to survive the fury of the French government and the indignation of the French press. During his fort-night at sea the French navy had expended a great deal of their tax-payers' money on a fruitless search for him, and had then declared him missing presumed dead. When he eventually made it back to Paris the French press largely lambasted him as a fraud, and he spent a great deal of time trying to persuade them otherwise. The Russians signed a document saying that he had indeed crossed the Bering Straits, and eventually he and his own people were able to make their peace.

Postscript

Of course a showman never lies down, and a year later the Baron was in the news again. On one side

Baron Arnaud de Rosnay prior to racing Ken Winner across the English Channel for $5000. They both had to be rescued by helicopter, and they both lost their boards.

of the world he was busy organizing a professional 'Speed Crossing' be-tween the Hawaiian islands of Maui (his adopted home) and Molokai, while on the other he had to be rescued from the middle of the English Channel after challenging Ken Winner to a race from Britain to France. The prize was $5000 – and neither of them won it!

In the summer of 1982 the Baron had another go at the English Chan-nel, and broke the record sailing from France to England, and then back again. No doubt we will hear of many more of his feats in years to come.

Chronology

1979

February. Ken Winner windsurfs 100 miles along the Florida coast in 6 hours 49 minutes.

August. Baron Arnaud de Rosnay windsurfs across the Bering Straits from Alaska to Siberia. He covers 85 miles in 8 hours without assistance.

November. Sergio Ferrero of Italy windsurfs 150 miles from Ibiza to Barcelona.

December. Frederic Beauchêne of France windsurfs in hops around Cape Horn, with a support team and two inflatable boats.

Christian Marty (no doubt taking advantage of an airline employee's cheap flight) windsurfs 100 miles from Guadeloupe to Martinique, in preparation for his 1982 Atlantic crossing.

1980

June. Christian Marty windsurfs 105 miles from Nice to Corsica.

September. Baron Arnaud de Rosnay covers 750 miles of the Pacific in 13 days unassisted. He is not popular with the French navy.

October. Anne Gardner and Jack Wood windsurf across the 70 miles of the world's highest stretch of water, Lake Titicaca in South America.

1981

September. An English team windsurfs around the UK on a Sea Panther board.

December. Frederic Giraldi of France windsurfs from the Canaries to Guadaloupe. He intended staying on his board all the way across, but resorted to sleeping on his support boat each night.

1982

January. Christian Marty windsurfs the Atlantic from Africa to America without leaving his board.

Fred Beauchêne silhouetted against the might of Cape Horn (above and below). With a little sponsorship from Dufour he had a full support team in inflatable rubber boats, but windsurfing around Cape Horn still remains a unique and solitary achievement – the North-West Passage must be next.

New Ideas

The windsurfing concept isn't just limited to use on water, and even when it is, it can find some strange new directions, as the picture opposite shows.

Windsurfing got popular about the same time as skateboarding though happily it's here to stay, rather than being just a short-lived craze. However the principles behind the two sports are similar – speed, sensation, and balance – and in the past 10 years various 'landsurfers' have been produced which combine the windsurfer rig with a skateboard or something similar.

The most basic combination of a mast foot on a standard skateboard proved unworkable – too difficult to control, with far too much strain on the tiny wheels – and the manufacturers who entered this field were forced to seek a considerably more sophisticated design solution.

In most cases the basic principles of a skateboard have been retained. The board should be steered by banking it, and this turns the wheels on the damped steering system.

The variations are in the size and shape of the board and its wheels. Obviously a light board with small wheels giving minimum skin resistance will travel very fast, but will only do so on a perfect surface such as tarmac, and by virtue of its size will be very difficult to sail.

A larger board will take more wind to get moving and will build up speed more slowly, but is bound to be easier to control and will be far more at home when the surface is of variable solidity, as on a beach. The softer the sand, the broader the wheels need to be, and footballs mounted on bearings have proved very successful. Taken to its limit, Baron Arnaud de Rosnay's Speed Sail (see pages 154–159) with which he windsurfed the Sahara was a nine foot long skateboard with 4 + 4 wheels – he added the second set to make eight in all for very soft sand.

Sailing a Landsurfer

The most obvious difference between landsurfing and windsurfing is falling off. It's hard, and if it's on tarmac it will be very hard and you'll be going very fast. Obviously you have to wear all the skateboarding gear – crash hat, knee and elbow pads – and take great care not to break your neck.

The technique is also different. Compared to water the surface is smooth and there is far less skin friction. You travel a lot faster in the same amount of wind, and consequently the 'apparent wind' changes direction very rapidly. Once you build up speed, you always need to sheet the sail in tight, and so the rig needs to be much flatter than on a conventional windsurfer. It needs to be designed specifically for the job, and will generally feature a stiff alloy spar, a short foot, and a strop rather than a wishbone which will make it much easier to sheet the sail over the centreline of the board.

On most landsurfers, raking the rig fore and aft plays a minor part in steering. Instead, the board is steered by banking it, which turns the axles of the front wheels. Gybing is relatively easy, but when it comes to tacking you need to take great care. On a windsurfer you come to a virtual dead stop as the nose passes through the eye of the wind. However on a landsurfer you carry on moving with little loss of speed. You tack through an arc, and it's unnerving when you move round the front of the mast to change sides, facing backwards and still travelling at 20 miles per hour!

On Ice and Snow

If a windsurfer rig can be used on land it can obviously be used on ice, and the Russians are forerunners in this part of the game. They favour small boards of around two-and-a-half foot maximum length fitted with ice runners, and often use solid wing rigs to cope with the immense speeds they run at. 50 mph+ is the norm, so it's not a sport for the fainthearted.

Using a windsurfer rig on snow is somewhat different, as there is much more skin friction and obviously the speeds are lower. However, enthusiasts in North America and Scandinavia have successfully mated rigs with skis and toboggans in much the same fashion.

Hydrofoils

The idea of the hydrofoil is that once a craft reaches an initial speed, it will 'lift out' and stand up on its foils, which have a far smaller wetted area than the hull itself.

The principle has been tried with limited success on windsurfers. They have problems reaching the required speed to 'lift out' due to the drag of the submerged foils, and then when the board does lift out, it becomes very difficult to control.

An interesting tandem-hydrofoil-proa was designed to overcome these problems – tandem for power; proa outrigger for stability – but met with limited success. It was named 'Sweeny' after its designer, Mike Todd.

Different Rigs

The windsurfer rig as developed and patented by Hoyle Schweitzer has remained much the same. The shaping and materials used may have improved, but it is still recognizably the 20 year old original.

Most of the rigs which are obviously rather different have been dreamt up by or resurrected by 'patent beaters'. Thus Newman Darby's square-rigger type of windsurfer sail was proudly held up to the German courts as 'prior art' – ie someone else had invented the windsurfer before Schweitzer. This

Jim Drake introduced the 'Wingsurfer' at the 1982 Pan Am Cup – you need a strong pair of arms for it.

attempt was unsuccessful, but other people have set out to design rigs specifically to circumvent the patent. Such rigs do the same job while wriggling round the intricacies of the law.

We have therefore seen some very odd variations on the conventional wishbone. There was the straight sided one that was popular in the UK for a few years; another that looked like a hair pin with curly sides; and a single straight boom that sliced the sail in half (Peter Chilvers, the man who was held by the British courts to have sailed a 'sailboard' before Schweitzer, developed a rig based on this principle, claiming its superiority to the conventional rig. However there has been no sign of it being a commercial success.)

A further answer to the patent question was a four sided 'quadsail' (another British invention) which allowed the wishbone to be attached to the leading edge of the sail without touching the mast. Like most of the other 'patent beaters' it worked reasonably well, without demonstrating any particular superiority over the Schweitzer rig.

Back to Drake

Jim Drake is generally credited as the man who invented it all (see pages 12–13) and at Hawaii in 1982 he looked ready to start it all again, with a rig that would certainly beat the patent, and looked as though it had been developed from a hangglider. The locals tried it hooked on and hanging in, but the likeable and easy-going Mr Drake had his tongue firmly in his cheek all the time. We'll have to wait and see what he comes up with in the future.

Left: Another shot of the 'Wingsurfer'. The sailor-aviator would probably find sailing with it a lot easier if he was clipped on by a harness.

Above: A tricycle landsurfer with footstraps and big tyres – the latter are vital if it is going to be used on any soft surface such as a beach.

Steering is normally by damping. You lean the landsurfer into the wind to head up towards it; you lean it away from the wind to head away from it. Inclining the rig plays very little part in governing which direction you steer. Tacking is tricky. With so little 'foredeck', perhaps a duck tack is the best answer.

Where It's At

Windsurfing is best experienced when the weather and water are warm, and when there's a good breeze. For those who haven't tried it, windsurfing without a wetsuit is a thousand times better than cold, clammy, constricting rubber.

There are now holiday packages for windsurfers available in most of the desirable corners of the world. These vary from the very simple and very cheap, to the sophisticated and very expensive. Either way, you should check out whether it's a holiday that just happens to include windsurfing, or one that has been specifically designed around the needs of the sport – otherwise, you may be disappointed.

Occasionally you will be expected to take your own boards and equipment, but usually the board at least will be provided. In this case it is important to check that the sort of boards you like sailing are available, and just how much use of them will be included in the cost of the package. Remember that being saddled with some ancient board is almost as bad as twiddling your thumbs on the beach while someone hogs the one you want to try.

Holidays are excellent for learning windsurfing. Two uninterrupted weeks of perfect conditions are enough to get anyone past the basics, but you should ensure the teaching is to the standard you require. It is best by far if a proper IWS course is on offer (see pages 33ff) which will give you a recognized certificate. In some countries you may actually need this certificate before they allow you to go windsurfing.

Some holidays also cater for advanced learning – ie getting you through the Force 4+ barrier and on as far as wave jumping techniques, with some tuition thrown in. This will enable you to try sailing in more difficult conditions without having to buy expensive specialist equipment.

Right: Florida in the the Gulf of Mexico. As a simple rule of thumb, anywhere with nice big palm trees is OK when it comes to windsurfing – anywhere with sharks is not so good.

Below: The Island of Hydra in the Aegean Sea off Greece. Lovely and warm, and in the hot summer months the Meltemi is a reliable afternoon wind, blowing at Force 4 or 5 every day. Hydra hosted the Windsurfer World Championship in the autumn of 1979 — at that time of the year the weather was unfortunately less pleasant.

Regattas

Regatta sailing is a great way to travel. Most of the major class associations run their European and World events in exotic places, and have special cheap packages which enable competitors to turn them into two week family holidays.

You will invariably find that boards and rigs are provided gratis or for a nominal fee by the one-design associations. After the event is over this equipment is normally sold off very cheap for those who want to take advantage of it.

The package will also include travel, hotel, and a succession of parties, barbecues, discos, etc, making the cost almost inclusive.

Sun Care

Many windsurfers live in northern climes and are not used to fair weather sailing. Therefore some sensible precautions need to be taken.

Windsurfing is a great way to get a suntan. The sail reflects the bright light (if you want to get really brown, a white sail is *de rigeur*) which also bounces back off the water, while the wind keeps you cool. But it is also a great way to get burnt, and it is no good ruining your holiday by needing a week's recovery after one day's wind-surfing.

If it's really hot, protect your body, and it may be advisable to wear a hat as well. Most important of all, don't burn your feet. Standing on a gleaming white board with your feet half submerged can lead to critical sunburn, and you should either wear some footwear, or a waterproof sun tan cream that has a powerful screen. Some brands are very effective. It takes a long time

Just look at that surf! This is Hookipa Beach on the island of Maui, one of the Hawaiian group. If anything it's rated more highly than Oahu, where the Pan Am Cup is held.

to wash off, but take care not to rub it off if you're pushing your feet in and out of footstraps.

Transporting a Board

When you go off to your favourite hotspot, you may well prefer to take your own board rather than risk hiring.

Most of the airlines will carry boards, but just how easy this is varies from place to place and from airline to airline. It used to be the case that you could simply turn up at the airport with your board under your arm, and they would take it as part of the baggage allowance.

However, now that windsurfing is a lot more popular, you stand a pretty good chance of getting turned away at the check-in. You should always check with the airline in advance what facilities they have for boards, and then you won't be disappointed. Some will still take them as baggage, while others want a fat fee for taking them cargo (and one month in advance). Hopefully the rest have special deals available.

Take care when you trust your board to the tender mercies of the airport ground staff. To them it's a big solid lump, and if you want it to arrive in one piece, make sure it's well wrapped in expanded polythene sheeting with all the accessories taped firmly to the board. Also make sure you understand the insurance liability before you travel.

Europe

Most Europeans head for the Mediterranean, where the summer guarantees sun, even if the wind isn't more forthcoming.

Generally, the further east you go, the more reliable the wind will be. In the hottest months the Greek Meltemi blows up every afternoon, reaching Force 4 or more and blowing steadily until the evening. It is predictable and you know what to expect, but further west the wind can strike with unexpected severity. Any sailor who has tried the coastal area around Marseilles knows how quickly the Mistral transforms the placid Mediterranean, and it is very easy to get caught out.

Further north, the great Euro-

A Thai duet on two Thai boards in Israel! This is Nahariya, just near the border on the Israeli Mediterranean coast, during the Open Class World Championship in 1980. The competitors were protected by gunboats!

pean windsurfing centre is Lake Garda near Milan in Italy. Every summer weekend it's liable to be saturated by around 6000 windsurfers, the majority of whom are German, Austrian, and, of course, Italian.

They come for the thermal winds that are caused by the mountains that encircle the lake. Every morning there's the Vento which seldom blows more than Force 3 and is ideal for beginners, while every afternoon the Ora takes over for the better sailors with Force 5–8.

North again, and the West Country of England has the reputation for the best wave sailing in Europe – but it's not reliable.

The Atlantic

The Canary Islands and Lanzarotte in particular are considered good strong wind/sun areas, benefiting from Trade Winds all the year round.

On the opposite side of the Atlantic, the West Indies are just a little bit further south, so they get rather more sun with the same predictable wind pattern. The French islands (Guadeloupe, Martinique, etc) are all well known for windsurfing.

USA

The warm weather states of California and Florida are both popular, with San Francisco Bay having a particularly good summertime reputation, even though the water stays cold. For winter sun, visits over the Mexican border are recommended, with Baja and Cancun both being good.

Hawaii (see pages 26–29) is, of course, the American Number One, whether it's winter or summer. It may be expensive (to get to and live in), overcrowded (on the capital island of Oahu at least), and with a wind that isn't always predictable, but it still continues to attract the stars.

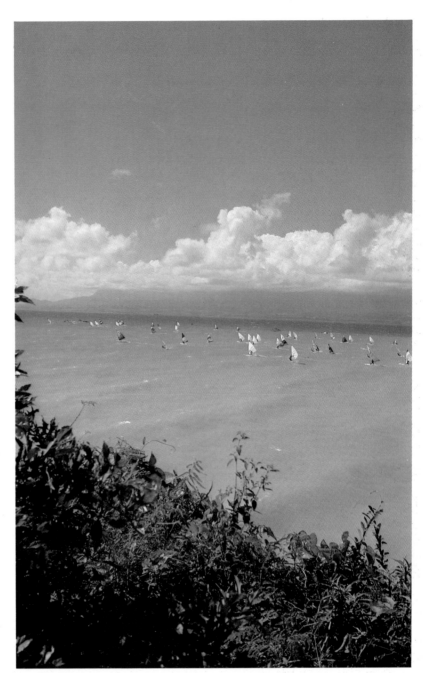

Australia

Australia now has some of the world's best strong wind sailing, while a short hop to Thailand's Siam Cup must be the best way to spend each Christmas (although the wind can be unpredictable). In fact the list is endless. Wherever there's sun, sea, and a good wind, there will be windsurfers.

Guadeloupe in the French West Indies was the venue of the 1979 Open Class World Championship, and is pretty desirable by any standards. The food is better than on the British or American islands, and the girls are a lot prettier, although it does tend to be more expensive. Martinique is its smart neighbour.

Photography with Alastair Black

Surely one of the sporting world's most spectacular subjects, wind-surfing has to be also one of the most challenging. As a professional photographer I have to be armed with every available weapon for this challenge or I cannot hope to cover the full range of options available. But virtually every reader is going to be an amateur with a limited budget for photo equipment, so how can I be helpful and at the same time practical within the limitations?

Probably the most helpful suggestion will be – think carefully about each picture. Do not just point and shoot. It is so easy to look with your eyes, then lift up the camera, peer through the viewfinder, and see what you want to see – not what is really there. Even after years of looking through finders I still have to tell myself positively to see the image critically, to remember how small that sailboard in the centre really is in relation to the total picture area, to spot the distractions around it, to think of the lighting situation as it will affect the result. And above all, not to take a photo if the result will be dull and uninteresting.

Of course, what is dull to one person can be fascinating to another, so I should not really discourage any kind of image creation. Certainly there is no better way to learn than by making mistakes!

Equipment

It really is an impossibility to produce any passable photograph with commonly used snapshot camera intended for family snaps of the baby and Aunt Ethel. These are ingenious, clever pieces of equipment, but simply lack lenses of adequate focal length even to remotely fill sufficient space in the picture area with a sailboard. There could be the odd occasion when an opportunity comes along for the distance to be short enough. But on the whole, forget it.

To begin producing good wind-surfing photos, a single lens reflex camera with interchangeable lenses is essential, and it should not only offer automatic exposure which can be invaluable at the right time, but manual over-ride also. There are plenty of makes which are adequate, reliable and easy to use. No particular recommendations here but all the well-known names produce good models.

A zoom lens, from 70–200 mm focal length or thereabouts, will be invaluable, as it offers more scope for 'filling the frame' from varying distances. If a shorter focal length zoom, say 35–70 mm is added, then you have no excuses – well, not many.

The greatest difference between an amateur and a professional photographer is not necessarily the ability of the latter to produce good photos. It is the fact that the pro *must* produce good work each and every time, plus enough of it to satisfy the many markets waiting to

Above: Alastair Black threw up his living as a dentist to become an international yachting photographer. He's never looked back.

use it. So, as amateurs, it's a piece of cake. You have nothing to lose, can take chances, try any ideas and all you lose is a bit of film.

Now for a few guidelines on some basic essentials. I shall assume the reader has a knowledge of the mechanics of photography because this is not the place to start explaining about focal lengths, f-stops, film speeds and all the details involved with understanding how to generate reasonable photos. If that knowledge is absent, there are countless 'How To' photo books available, which will provide the necessary background information.

Right: The end of the day, using a UV filter which is enough to make the orange light at that time even stronger.

Films

I would suggest you use only reversal film, ie slides. Like most professionals I am a Kodachrome addict – generally 64 ASA – because it is so sharp, has good colour and can be processed anywhere. Black and white loses all the potential of colour. Colour negative film can only produce prints. Slides offer everything – good prints can now be made easily from them – they are necessary for all the repro-

duction you see in magazines and books – and they can be projected on to a screen. Another advantage is that every frame can be easily seen to compare your work without having to obtain a print first.

Using colour calls for sunshine shooting, because there is little that is more boring that a white sailed windsurfer on a grey and windless day. For years I have campaigned against these dull, tedious, drab, white sails in what is essentially a

bright, extrovert, exciting sport.

So try to save your film and efforts for a sunny day preferably with a brisk wind. But even when winds are gentle there is plenty you can produce. Late in the day, in particular, is best. From late afternoon on to sunset in the summertime can produce much warmer colours, and if the sun is low it makes a wonderful background to shoot into – lots of sparkle on the water with that golden orb itself making the perfect backdrop for a windsurfer (even one with a white sail).

When using colour film at sea it is necessary to use an ultraviolet or skylight filter to cut down the overall blue cast in these conditions. A skylight has more red in its effect, so outside the couple of hours around the mid-day the clouds can become a little too pink and the warming-up effect a bit excessive as sunset draws nearer. For that reason I use U.V. constantly, and even it can turn an evening scene into an orange glow that is much more vivid than the eye can perceive.

If using B.W. film, a yellow or orange filter will add greatly to the contrast between white sails or clouds and sky.

For really strong colour effects, a polarizing filter used to its maximum potential will bring out all the colours with an unreal vividness.

Some people like this but I seldom use polarizers as the results can be too unnatural – and you lose two stops in speed because of these filters' light absorbing nature.

Nowadays there are also hundreds of 'creative' filters in a variety of systems. Several can be useful in windsurfing photography but in general no filter will make a silk purse out of a sow's ear, so if your basic shot is second rate it will still be second rate 'with filter effect'.

Remember again – think before you shoot.

*　　*　　*

Having covered what can be in and what can be on the camera, it is time to consider where it is going to be when the pictures are being made. Ignoring aerial photography, which is strictly professional, three other possible bases for your camera exist: On the land. On the water. In the water.

Above: If this had been taken from the other side of the windsurfers, the effect would have been flat and uninteresting – always think about how a different position has a different image.

Right: Keep your eyes open for the unexpected. No photo skill is needed apart from observation and the ability to focus quickly when using a telephoto lens – and remember the exposure.

On the Land

Obviously this limits the angles. All the action is going on outside your control and pictures have to be made within these limitations.

If your stretch of land is on the south of the water, then all the photos are going to have normal 'over-the-shoulder' lighting and there is no chance of sparkly backlit water photos.

If it is to the west or east of the water then the lighting will vary according to the time of day, so if sailing is going on all day and you can choose when to shoot, think about when conditions may be best or when they provide the effects you most want.

If your base faces south over the water, most times are going to offer the chance for backlit photos only. This is pictorially the most attractive, but it means that the subject's face and the details are usually in shadow so there will be problems if the object is to show people and personalities. Exposures can be longer, of course, to allow the darker shadow areas to be clear, but this means the bright water becomes a 'burned-out', over-exposed area. There is no compromise. You have to decide the priority and expose accordingly. If left to auto-exposure, the dominant area will determine the exposure and if that is bright, the shadows will become obscure black areas.

Working from land, the distance from the subject is the greatest problem and the absence of powerful enough telephoto lenses limits possibilities. If using a zoom, then 200 mm is about the limit and most sailing must be relatively close. Longer – 300 mm, 400 mm – lenses are available at relatively modest cost, and converters which double the effective focal length can be

Sitting in a rescue boat at the leeward mark with an 80–200 mm zoom lens gives plenty of chances to take photos of the action.

added. The price to pay for a 2 times converter in terms of extra power is the loss of 2 f. stops on exposure and darkening of the viewfinder image which makes focusing harder. For any long telephoto lenses a tripod is essential.

500 mm mirror lenses are not too expensive and are light to handle. Although having a fixed f. stop they offer probably the best compromise.

On the Water

Unless spiritually endowed, you are going to need a power boat to provide a platform. To have any mobility it *must* be driven with consideration for all and any sailors. Primary considerations are: no interference if there is racing going on, and *no* hazard, with a clear look out at all times. You can circle around a race course and choose the shooting angle. Apply the same principles as from land. Any lens can be used and only the distance is your guiding factor. Remember again that the image in the viewfinder is true. Don't see it as you *want* to see it.

Best for exciting photos is to work with a friend sailing his board for the pictures. (They all love posing!) He can sail at, around or behind your boat.

Remember the hazards of salt water on your equipment. Wear an anorak which can cover your camera. Turn your back to the spray most of the time. At the end of the day, if spray has got at the gear, I always wipe it thoroughly with a wet, fresh water cloth and dry off as soon as I get back to base.

In the Water

No doubt you have looked at lots of sailboarding pictures and given some thought to how they were produced. Almost every time the

Shooting from the land gives a high vantage point when you use a long tripod mounted telephoto lens.

most exciting shots are made from an in-water position. Obviously, this calls for waterproof equipment so unless you have a waterproof housing for the normal SLR cameras it is necessary to have an actual waterproof camera. I use the long-established Nikonos, either the manual III or automatic IVA and prefer the control available on the older one. But apart from its bulk I would rather work with a proper waterproof housing which permits choice of lenses on the SLR camera, with a motor drive to ensure no good opportunities are missed. At the same time one must remember to conserve film – it can be a long swim and a hassle to get back ashore just to replace film.

Unless you are a good swimmer and feel totally at home in the water forget about this kind of windsurf photography. It's a waste of time if more effort goes into the swimming than the photography!

In Hawaii, the local surf photographers have the advantage of many years familiarity and experience against us very occasional in-water Europeans. And if the waves are difficult with coral near the surface one can feel very much a foreign body in the sea. In the UK and Europe of course, a full wet suit is generally necessary. Without waves a buoyancy aid gives helpful height in the water. Dive fins are almost a necessity for manoeuvrability.

Camera exposures are best set manually to suit the angle to sun you are choosing to shoot. A good spit on the protective glass now and again helps the salt water to slide off the lens protecting surface.

The services of a *competent, reliable* sailing subject are also a necessity. Remember it can be dangerous with a board tearing past (and hopefully not over) you.

Finally, remember that in the end it's not your equipment or the subject that makes the shot – it's how you shoot it.

Manufacturing Techniques

Most boards are made from an outer plastic skin completely filled with foam. This is usually polyurethane, mixed from two constituents which expand rapidly on contact. A less usual alternative is polystyrene foam, which is lighter but weaker, and is generally reserved for racing boards.

The foam is usually injected after the skin has been made, and gives the board its shape, rigidity, and buoyancy. The distribution of the foam and its bond to the skin is critical. With enough hard use the foam in the best-made board will begin to separate, and will then start to break up.

The three most popular skin materials are polyethylene, ABS and glassfibre.

Polyethylene

It is generally agreed that this is the toughest material, but there are problems. Tooling costs are higher than any other process (except polypropylene), and for some manufacturers it has taken several years to sort out an acceptable finish – they have been plagued by boards full of bumps, hollows, and weakness where the skin has run too thin.

It is easy to see whether a board has a 'fair' (ie smooth) finish, but not whether the polyethylene is thick enough in the right places, or indeed of the right quality.

Like most materials, polyethylene is available in different grades (generally relating to density of the molecular structure), and a low density board (cheap) may well run into problems such as warping when there are extreme changes of heat.

There are two main methods of polyethylene manufacture: roto- and blow-moulding.

Roto-moulding

The number of roto-moulding plants is limited by their cost. One machine producing two boards at a time will cost around $250,000!

The Dutch Windsurfer manufacturer Ten Cate is a leader in this field, and the way they roto-mould their Windsurfer boards is similar to techniques used by other manufacturers. The process starts with two sets of board-shaped metal moulds, which are mounted back to back. Each mould has a top and a bottom half, and the polyethylene powder is poured into the bottom half, before the top half is clamped on to it.

The moulds are then placed in a gas fired oven which heats them for around 20 minutes at 200°C. After the oven the moulds go to the cooler for a 15 minute blast of cold air. They are then opened, and the plastic skins literally ripped out by hand – they look rather like limp white sausages. The moulds then need minimal preparation with a release agent for the next cycle.

The plastic skins are placed in a foaming box – a metal mould which is the shape of the final board. Pre-measured foam is shot in through a hole in the stern for around 30 seconds, and then left to expand and settle for 15 minutes. Any excess is normally allowed to escape – usually through the hole which will take the towing eye.

The board can then be removed from the foaming box. Excess polyethylene is trimmed by hand, and striping and detailing added before final packaging.

Blow-moulding

In this method the polyethylene is blown into the mould, rather as one would blow up a balloon. The theory is that this gives greater control over the spread of the thickness of the plastic.

ABS

ABS is a plastic material which is probably the most popular amongst board manufacturers. Like polyethylene it comes in different grades, and once again it is very difficult for the buyer to sort out what quality he is getting.

ABS plastic is used by such popular marques as Klepper, Jet, and Sainval.

It is not as tough a material as polyethylene, but it is far easier for the manufacturer to get a good finish with it.

The process

There are various ways of producing an ABS board, and the French and German manufacturers have always been at the forefront of developments.

The first ABS boards were produced by heating a flat sheet of ABS, and then lowering it down so that it could envelop a metal mould. Like polyethylene, this led to problems with thinness and thickness. A better and more sophisticated technique has now been developed whereby the heated sheet is blown up on to the mould. The plastic skins forming the hull bottom and top are then taken from the moulds, and hand trimmed to remove the rough edges. The essential fittings (mast foot, daggerboard well, and skeg box units) are then bonded into place, before the two halves are joined. The most primitive method is to simply glue them and cap the join with a plastic strip; a more sophisticated method is an H-shaped plastic joint which fits into the two halves.

The board is then placed in a foaming box, with the remainder of the process being similar to the finishing of polyethylene or glassfibre boards – it is only the skin material which is essentially different.

ASA

ASA is a variation on ABS, mainly developed by the German Sailboard marque.

They use a rather different and highly sophisticated method of constructing their boards, which was first introduced in 1982.

They blow their foam first, and then mould the ASA around it compressing the whole lot together in a mould. The great advantage is that there is then no hull/deck join, as the skin is one continuous moulding without a break.

Glassfibre

Glassfibre is the most labour-intensive of the three materials. It is therefore the easiest to control, and has initial tooling costs which are a fraction of setting up polyethylene or ABS plants in both time and money. It is therefore favoured by the smaller manufacturers, and is more suitable for short-lived production runs of up-to-the-minute specialist boards (Open Class roundboard racing or wave jumping), which must be put into production quickly, and may be outdated in nine months. It is an ideal material for getting a good finish and controlling the weight, strengths, and weaknesses of a board, but as a shock absorbing skin is far more fragile than the others.

The process

Glassfibre boards are made in moulds, similar to polyethylene or ABS, and the process is much the same as for yacht building.

The gel coat, which will become the shiny outer skin, is first sprayed or brushed into the mould – it is like a thick paint. Then the glass mat is laid in place, with extra thicknesses at the stress points, and the polyester resin is brushed in which turns it into hard glassfibre. Alternatively the glassfibre can be shot with a 'gun', that chops small strands of glass mat and sprays them at high speed on to the mould, together with a stream of resin.

In his search for strength with low weight, the builder can opt for:

1. Epoxy resin. Longer curing and more difficult to work with than polyester resin, but the same strength for less weight.

Mistral work with epoxy resin on their Naish and Competition Light boards. Like Sailboard they begin by blowing a foam blank, which is then covered with glass mat and epoxy resin, before being put in a mould to cure. It is then removed and spray finished.

2. Hollow boards. A hollow board reinforced with ply 'stringers' and 'frames' will have great rigidity. Foam blocks must be inserted to provide buoyancy, but they have no structural value. Racing boards such as the Parker Turbo opt for this technique.

The main disadvantage of hollow boards is that they will be prone to leaks.

3. Foam sandwich. Usually used in conjunction with hollow boards.

A foam sandwich filling between the layers of glass mat gives the board an extra strong skin with little increase in weight. However, hard use can lead to delamination of the foam from the mat.

4. Exotic materials. Kevlar is stronger than glass mat, but more expensive and much more difficult to work with. Carbon fibre can be used as a strengthening material in places of stress, but has the same drawbacks.

Neither are allowed in the construction of Open Class Division 1 and 2 racing boards.

Other materials

Polypropylene

Polypropylene is a plastic which is used to make washing-up bowls! It was first used in a sailing context with the Topper dinghy, and then the first polypropylene board, the Dulfour Sun, was launched in 1981.

The tooling costs are immense, and the lead-up time of around 18 months is enough to put off most manufacturers. Who is going to predict which design will sell in thousands that far ahead? However, once in production the unit costs are appreciably lower than any other form of manufacture.

Wood

By definition wooden boards must be hand built.

A simple and cheap 'kit' method of construction is to make up a board with sheets of ply held together by glassfibre tape and copper wire 'stitches'. The disadvantages are that the ply sheets do not give much scope for shaping the board, which will be prone to leaks.

A far more complex alternative is to shape and glue thin sheets of ply laminate over a male mould. This is based on a classic method of dinghy construction, but has no conceivable advantages apart from producing a very beautiful board.

'Soft' boards

'Soft' boards are made of shaped sheets of polyethylene foam, laminated and pressed in a mould – the heat then forms a skin.

They are very light, and with their 'soft' finish ideal for playing around on. However, they are not very robust.

Manufacture of Fittings

Glassfibre masts are made up from pre-prepared glass and resin (usually polyester; occasionally epoxy) rolls, which are cut into mast-long lengths, and then wrapped around lightly heated stainless steel mandrils. These are placed in an oven for about 20 minutes, and the mast can then be slid off the mandril ready for use.

Alloy masts are made of tapered extrusions of aluminium. The wall thickness and diameter has a governing effect on the weight and bending characteristics of the mast.

Hull fittings

It is becoming increasingly common for all hull fittings and ancilliaries – mast foot and well, skeg box, daggerboard case, daggerboard, skeg, towing eye, etc – to be manufactured by outside contractors. They are usually moulded in plastics such as ABS, or polypropylene which is cheaper but has a weight penalty. The units are delivered ready to be bonded into the board.

Glossary

Note: Words in *italics* are explained elsewhere in the Glossary.

A

ABS
A plastic skin material used in the mass-production of boards.

Allround
An allround board is one that suits a wide variety of conditions. Usually this means that it is a *flatboard* which is suitable for learners, more experienced sailors, and *strong wind* sailing.

Apparent wind
The wind that is experienced by the sailor – different in direction and speed from the *true wind* experienced by a stationary observer.

ASA
A skin material similar to *ABS*.

B

Bale out
There comes a time when you're jumping off a wave and feel that it's mutually beneficial if you and your board part company. Don't let it come back down on top of you.

Battens
Flat pieces of flexible *fibreglass* used to support the *roach* of the sail.

Bearing away
Sailing away from the wind – normally by inclining the *rig* forwards.

Beating
'Beating to *windward*' – sailing as close to the wind as possible.

Beaufort Scale
Admiral Beaufort invented the Beaufort Scale, a measurement of wind speed based on *knots*. The Beaufort Scale is measured from Force 0 to Force 12.

Blank
A foam blank is roughly board shape and size. It is 'shaped' into a *custom* board. The foam is either polyurethane (more usual) or polystyrene.

Boardsailing
How to avoid saying windsurfing.

Bow
The front end of the board.

Break
General surfing term for the wave and where it starts breaking. 'Shorebreak' is where it hits the shore.

C

Camber
The amount of curve in the sail – whether it is trimmed full or flat.

Carbon fibre
Strengthening material used in the construction of exotic boards.

Carve
To 'carve a *gybe*' or 'carve a turn' – altering course at high speed, achieved by pushing on the *rail*.

Cavitation
The *skegs* and the back of the board cease to grip the water. The back of the board then slides away and *spins out*.

CE
The Centre of Effort – the fulcrum of the wind's power in the sail.

Chill factor
Getting cold due to the wind lowering your body temperature.

Chine
A flat surface, usually on the underside of the board.

Chord
An imaginary straight line drawn between the shortest distance from the *clew* of the sail to the *mast*.

Cleat
A small fitting used to secure a line. 'Clamcleats' are the popular sort, placed on the *wishbone* to secure the *outhaul* line.

Clew
The outer corner of the sail which is attached to the end of the *wishbone*.

Clew-first
To 'sail clew-first' – to sail with the *clew* pointing towards the wind. Used in *freestyle* and *strong wind* gybing techniques.

Close hauled
To sail as close to the wind as possible – beating, etc.

CLR
Centre of Lateral Resistance – the main point about which a board will resist and turn. In practice this usually means the *daggerboard*.

Custom
'Custom board' – hand made from a foam *blank*.

CYT
Superior cloth finish to *terylene* sails – normally used by racers.

D

Dacron
A type of *terylene* sailcloth.

Daggerboard
Large fin mid-way in the board, which is removable from the *daggerboard* case. Prevents the board going sideways.
  A *storm daggerboard* is much shorter, and makes the board easier to control in strong winds. Made in moulded plastic or laminated plywood.

Depression
Period of unsettled weather which normally means wind. Also called a *low*.

Displacement
'Displacement board' – loose term for board with rounded underwater shape to reduce *wetted area*. Usually refers to an *Open Class roundboard*.

Donkey kick
Kicking the back end of the board down when you jump off a wave, so the board goes into vertical takeoff.

Donkey's ear
Strong wind *skeg*, shaped as above.

Downhaul line
Attaches the *tack* of the sail to the *universal joint*.

Drake
Jim Drake probably did most to invent windsurfing.

Dry suit
A neoprene suit, with neck and wrist seals, that keeps the water out. For cold weather windsurfing.

Duck tack
Ducking under the *rig*, rather than walking round the front of it. You can also 'duck *gybe*'.

E

Epoxy resin
Superior resin used to 'cure' glass mat, Kevlar, etc. Difficult to work with.

Eye of the wind
The precise direction from which the wind is blowing.

F

Fathead
Strong wind sail with a full *head* supported by one or two *battens*. The theory is that you don't lose power down in the trough of waves, and can use a shorter *wishbone* for the same sail area. A 'fullhead' is the same four-sided shape, but is not so full at the top.

Fence
A fence or *cavitation* plate is a flat section like a small wing attached to a *skeg*. The theory is that it will disperse the passage of air bubbles which aerate the skeg and cause it to lose its grip on the water.

Fin
Another way of saying *skeg*. In strong wind terminology it would also refer to the *daggerboard*.

Floater
A board with enough buoyancy to carry your weight when stationary.

Foil
Like a V-shaped undercarriage. A hydrofoil will rise up and plane on its foil(s), requiring less power for more speed due to the diminished *wetted area*. Not very successful in windsurfing applications.

Foot
The bottom of the sail.

Footstraps
Straps to put your feet in so you keep connected to the board.

Freestyle
Performing tricks on a board, which in a competition must normally be compressed into a three minute routine.

Full
A sail is trimmed 'full' or 'flat' depending on the amount of *camber*.

Funboard
Generally means a *strong wind* board that is fun to sail.

G

Gasket
A rubber or plastic strip which keeps the water out of the *daggerboard case* when the daggerboard is fully retracted into the *hull*.

Gate start
One board sails across the fleet on *port tack* as the start gun is fired. To start, all the other boards must sail behind its stern. Normally used when there is a big *one-design* fleet.

Glassfibre
Glass mat which is 'cured' with resin. Used to make production boards, *custom* boards, and *masts*. Also called GRP and fibreglass.

Gybing
Altering course so the stern passes through the *eye of the wind*.

H

Harness
Used so that you can 'hook in' to a harness line either side of the *wishbone*.

Head
Top of the sail.

Head up
Sail up towards the wind – usually by inclining the *rig* aft towards the stern.

High aspect ratio
A HAR sail is tall and narrow – a low aspect ratio sail is flat and squat.

Hot dogging
The forerunner of *freestyle*.

Hull
The basic board, excluding the *rig*.

Hypothermia
Losing body heat due to exposure. A very dangerous condition.

I

IBSA
International Boardsailing Association.

Inhaul
The inhaul line attaches the *wishbone* to the *mast*.

Ins-and-outs
Strong wind competition in which boards *reach* up and down a course.

IWS
International Windsurfing Schools.

IYRU
International Yacht Racing Union.

J

Jolly good time
What we have when the wind blows hard.

K

Kanger's cock
Obscene Australian vernacular referring to a *strong wind skeg* shaped as the above.

Kevlar
Vaguely 'exotic' material with stronger properties than glass mat. Tends to be much more expensive and is difficult to work with.

Knots
Nautical miles per hour. A nautical mile is 2000 yards (1.85 km) rather than the more familiar 1760.

L

Lamination
Sticking materials together. Glass mat is laminated with resin to make a board; sheet ply is laminated with glue to make a *daggerboard*.

Le Mans start
The racers stand at the water's edge. When the start gun goes they launch their boards, jump on, and sail off. Normally used to start a *long distance race* – it is spectacular to watch.

Leash
You must have a leash connecting the *rig* to the board in case the *mast foot* pulls out.

Leech
The edge of the sail between the *head* and the *clew*.

Leeward
The side of the board the wind is blowing to. Opposite to *windward*.

Leeway
'Making leeway' – the amount the board moves sideways, or to *leeward*.

Lifejacket
A lifejacket will float you face up, and help prevent you from drowning if you are knocked out. A 'buoyancy aid' will usually float you face down – most buoyancy in *harnesses* falls into this category.

Lip
The 'lip of the wave' – the crest when it's just breaking.

Long distance race
A 'marathon' over at least 10 miles, hopefully more like 25 miles. Organizers try to include long reaching legs.

Long John
The popular windsurfing *wetsuit* – one-piece with long legs and no arms. You can wear a 'bolero' jacket on top.

Low
A *depression* – unsettled weather and wind.

Luff
The edge of the sail from the *head* to the *tack*. Next to the 'luff sleeve'.

Luff perpendicular
The measurement between the *wishbone* slot and the *clew*. Used by sailmakers.

Luffing
Heading up into the wind; heading up so that the wind strikes the *leeward* side of the sail; letting out the sail so that the wind does likewise. To 'luff a competitor' is to head up and force him to sail higher than he wishes to during a race.

M

Marginal sail
A sail for use when it's blowing too hard for a full size *regatta* sail. Normally straight or hollow leeched without *battens*.

Mast
Either made out of *glassfibre* or alloy – usually of uniform length.

Mast foot
Fits into the mast foot well, and is normally permanently attached to the *universal joint*. Every manufacturer seems to have a different fitting.

Maxi
A sail of 7 square metres or more, used for light conditions.

Munched
Eg 'He was munched by a wave'.

Mylar
Sailcloth made from a plastic film – only intended for light winds.

N

Neoprene
Fabric used for *wetsuits*, boots, gloves, etc. If it's unlined it's warmer (on the water off a duck's back principle) but prone to tearing.

Non-slip
Most boards have non-slip finishes moulded into the deck surface. They vary considerably, and can be improved by non-slip paint, or board *wax*.

Nose
Front end, or *bow* of the board.

O

Offshore wind
Wind blowing away from the shore.

Olympic triangle
The normal race course for boards, with three equal legs and 60 degree turns at each mark. Normal length of each leg is around one mile for an international event. The fleet usually sails round the triangle, followed by a 'sausage' leaving out the wing mark.

One-design
A class of identical boards – eg the *Windsurfer* Regatta.

Onshore wind
Wind blowing on to the shore.

Open class
Different boards racing together to the same design and construction rules. Open Class Division 1 is for flatboards; Open Class Division 2 is for roundboards.

Outhaul
Line to pull the *clew* of the sail out to the end of the *wishbone*.

P

Patent
Hoyle *Schweitzer* patented the concept of the *windsurfer*, and has chased his adversaries through the courts ever since.

Pentathlon
A *regatta* where five events count towards an overall prize; normally triangle racing, *long distance race*, *freestyle*, *slalom*, and *ins-and-outs*.

Pintail
A board designed for *strong winds* with a tapering *stern* for better control.

Plane
To skim across the water, rather than sailing through it.

Polyethylene
Plastic skin material used to mass produce boards. Polypropylene is similar, but different.

Polystyrene/polyurethane
Two types of foam used for providing the solid filling of boards.

Pop-out
A mass production board. It 'pops-out' of a mould.

Port
Left (looking forward). Indicated by the colour red.

Pumping
Pumping the rig back and forth creates wind in the sail and gives the board a lot of extra speed. However in IYRU racing you are only allowed 'three pumps to promote planing' – deciding who is and who isn't within the rules leads to a lot of protests and bad feeling.

Purling
Sticking the nose of the board into the wave and invariably going head over heels.

Q

QED
A *radical freestyle* demonstration.

R

Radical
US windsurfing expression ('I was putting in some really radical jumps – was I 50 or 60 feet clear?')

Rail
The side of the board. 'Riding the rail' is standing on the side.

Railing
Sailing along, with the board slightly on its side, induced by the push of the *mast foot* and the aquaplaning effect of the *daggerboard*. This technique is positively encouraged by *roundboard* sailors on upwind legs, as it reduces the *wetted area* of the board.

Reaching
Sailing with the wind on the beam – ie with the wind at or near 90 degrees to the board's course. You can sail a close reach, a beam reach, and a broad reach.

Regatta
A meeting with a series of races. A 'regatta sail' is a loose description of a sail which fits within the *Open Class* regatta norm – eg around 6.3 sq m

Resin
Turns glass mat into *glassfibre*.

Rig
Everything above the level of the *universal joint* (*mast*, sail, *wishbone* etc.)

Roach
The area of the sail which is supported by the *battens* – ie anything outside a straight line from the *head* to the *clew*.

Rocker
Curvature in the fore and aft plane of a board – a board that is absolutely flat underneath has no rocker (or 'scoop').

Roto-moulding
A method of moulding *polyethylene* boards, by rotating and rocking the moulds.

Roundboard
A racing board with an underwater profile that is round, and therefore cuts down *wetted area*, but is unstable. Normally refers to an *Open Class* Division 2 board.

Running
Sailing with the wind directly, or almost directly behind.

S

Sandwich
'Foam sandwich construction' has a skin made of two very thin skins (*glassfibre* or *Kevlar*) sandwiching a layer of foam around 1 cm thick. The board will normally be hollow, and this construction method enables it to be very strong and light.

Schweitzer
Hoyle Schweitzer helped invent the windsurfer with Jim *Drake*. He then patented it.

Scoop
Rocker at the nose of the board.

Set
Two waves, from crest to crest, travelling together.

Shaper
A person who shapes a foam *blank* into a board. He uses a saw, a plane, and a sanding tool.

Shims
Friction pads to ensure the *daggerboard* fits tightly in its case.

Shockcord
Elasticated cord that prevents the sailor losing the *uphaul*.

Simulator
A shore-bound *windsurfer* mounted on a turntable. Used for teaching by the *IWS* system.

Sinker
A board that sinks beneath you when stationary.

Skeg
Small fin at the *stern* of a board, to keep it sailing straight.

Slalom
A *regatta* knock-out competition in which two competitors *gybe* and *tack* round a small course.

Slot rubber
As with *gasket*. Keeps the water out of the *daggerboard* case when the daggerboard is retracted into the *hull*.

Speed trial
The fastest board over 500 metres during a timed run.

Spin-out
See *cavitation*.

Spreader bar
An aluminium bar which you wear across your chest to spread the load of the *harness*.

Starboard
Right (looking forward). Indicated by the colour green.

Stern
Back end of the board.

Storm daggerboard
A short *daggerboard* to overcome aquaplaning in strong winds.

Strong wind board
As for *funboard* – a board specifically for *strong winds*, normally with *footstraps*, big *skegs*, etc.

T

Tack
See Tacking. Alternatively the corner of the sail down by the *universal joint*.

Tacking
Altering course so the *nose* of the board passes through the *eye of the wind*. You do this if you want to sail towards the direction the wind is coming from. Could be called 'going about'.

Tail
Back end of the board.

Tandem
A *windsurfer* made for two.

Terylene
The material they make most sails from.

Tide
Coastal movement of the sea induced by pull of the sun and the moon. Tidal rip is when it runs extremely fast around a headland or in a confined area – it should be treated with respect by any sensible *windsurfer*.

Towing eye
In the *nose* of the board. To take a towing line, should you wish to be taken in tow.

Trim
To 'trim the sail' – letting it in and out as the wind changes.

True wind
The wind that is experienced by a stationary observer – different from the *apparent wind* experienced by someone on the move.

Tube
When a wave breaks on rapidly shelving ground, it creates a tube as the top curls over. The surfers travel along it.

U

Universal joint
Normally attached permanently to the *mast foot*, the UJ allows the *rig* to be swung through 360 degrees and inclined through a minimum of 180 degrees. The mast foot/universal joint unit is the adaptor between the rig and the board.

Uphaul
The rope used to pull the rig out of the water. It is attached to the *UJ* by *shockcord* – an alternative arrangement is an elasticated 'Hawaiian uphaul'.

V

Volume
The volume of the board determines its buoyancy, and to some extent its speed. If you weigh 300 pounds, make sure that you don't get a board that sinks under you.

W

Water start
Starting sailing when you're lying in the water, with the *rig* on top of you to *windward* of the board. Much used in *freestyle* and *de rigueur* for *sinkers* – it's not as easy as it might look.

Wax
Non-slip wax to help you stand on your board. ('Sex Wax' is a top selling brand.)

Weight groups
Division of competitors by weight for *triangle racing*. There are liable to be a maximum of four categories.

Wetted area
The area of the board that's in contact with the water. The less wetted area, the less drag, and the faster the board will go.

Windshift
A sudden shift in the wind's direction. When racing on upwind legs, competitors always *tack* on a windshift – it's the basis of tactics.

Windsurfer
Windsurfer with a capital W is a trade name – the original windsurfer invented by Hoyle *Schweitzer*. That's why some people talk about 'sailboards' and 'board sailing', rather than windsurfers and windsurfing.

Windward
The side of the board the wind is blowing from. Opposite to *leeward*.

Wipe-out
Taking an almighty fall.

Wishbone
The booms, made from two elliptical alloy tubes with plastic/nylon end fittings.

Appendices

Windsurfing Magazines

UK
On Board
Boardsailing International Ltd
28 Parkside
Wollaton
Nottingham.
Tel: 0602 226798

Windsurf
Ocean Publications Ltd
34 Buckingham Palace Rd
London SW1.
Tel: 01-828 4551

Surf News
PO Box 1
Hayling Island
Hampshire.

France
Planche
51 bis, Route de la Reine
92100 Boulogne/Billancourt

Planche No 1
75 Rue D'Amsterdam
75008 Paris.

Planche à Voile
15 Rue d'Argenteuil
75001 Paris.

Wind
28 Rue des Petites-Ecuries
75010 Paris.

Germany
Surf
Sachsenkamstrasse 19
Postfach 801008
8000 München 70.

Surf Journal
Ortlerster 8
8000 München 70.

Windsurfing Magazine
Ferdinand Maria Str 30
8000 München 19.

Netherlands
Surfsport
Z HD Hernn Paul Knopp
Postbus 50057
Netherlands 1305 AB Almere.

Surf Magazine
Z HD Herrn Van Wagensveld
Postbus 264
Netherlands 4200 Gorinchen.

Windsurfer
Herrn W Koesen
Herengracht 566
Amsterdam.

De Windsurfer
Z HD Hernn G Cooreman
Oosterdstraat 13
Netherlands 9000 Gent.

Japan
Hi Wind
Marine Planning Co Ltd
7F NS Building
2-2-3 Sarugaku-cho
Chiyoda-ku
Tokyo.

Austria
Ossterr Windsurfing Revue
Schidbauer
Schwarzenbergplatz 10
A-1040 Wien.

Sweden
Windsurfing
La Dore 65
Box 25033
10023 Stockholm.

USA
Windsurf
1955 W 190th St
Torrance
Ca 90509

Sailboarder
PO Box 1028
Dana Point
Ca 92629.

Board & Sail
PO Box 8108
Sacramento
Ca 95818.

Boardsailor
20 E Palm Avenue
Nokomis
Florida 33555.

Windsurfing Addresses

1. International Bodies
IYRU
60 Knightsbridge, London SW1.
Tel: 01-235 6221
The International Yacht Racing Union is the backbone of yacht racing throughout the world. With a few exceptions such as professional racing, most windsurfer races are run to IYRU rules.

IBSA
55 Avenue Kléber
75784 Paris Cedex 16
France.
Tel: 01 553 68 00.
The International Boardsailing Association founded the Open Class, doing all the initial development work on what is now Division 2. They have run the World and European championships for this class, but suffered a reversal in financial fortunes in 1982.

2. International Class Associations
IWCA
The Secretary
1955 West 190th St
Torrance Ca 90509
USA.
Tel: 213 515 4900.
The International Windsurfer Class Association has the greatest number of members who race one-design. Its World, European, and National championships are always extremely popular.

IWGCA
The Secretary
17/18 Sherman Avenue
Evanston
Illinois 60201
USA.
Tel: 312 475 3381.
The International Windglider Class is the only one-design association with membership behind the Iron Curtain, and was the IYRU's Olympic choice for 1984.

IMCO
Kerzer Sgracht 506
1017 E7
Amsterdam
Netherlands.
Tel: 2024 8961
The International Mistral Class Association (Mistral Light) is the youngest of the three international one-design associations.

3. International Regatta Organizers

Kailua Bay Windsurfing Association
PO Box 1224
Kailua
Hawaii 9 68 34.
Organizers of the famous Pan Am Cup. It's held each year in late March, but you should get your entry form the previous autumn.

Euro-Funboard Cup
Beethovenstrasse 10
8000 Munich 2
W. Germany.
The Euro-Funboard Cup is the major European strong wind series, with categories for both professional and amateur. It is run by Peter Brockhaus, a father figure of the Pan Am Cup.

WSP
30 Rochester Square
London NW1.
Windsurfing Professional organizes professional regattas which are run to its own racing rules. It tends to favour multi-discipline events.

4. U.S. Windsurfing Associations

Board Sailing USA
Brian Tulley, Director
Box 2157
Citrus Heights, California 95611
This association of boardsailors and operators runs a program of boardsailing fleets throughout the nation.

International Windsurfer Class Association
Kathy Truax, Coordinator
1955 West 190th Street
P.O. Box 2950
Torrence, California 90509

The 18 districts of the IWCA cover the entire continental U.S. as well as Puerto Rico, the Virgin Islands, Mexico, Canada, Argentina and Columbia. You can get the phone numbers and addresses of the district captain in your area by writing to the above address.

5. U.S. Windsurfing Schools

Boardsailing Instructor's Group
c/o Susan Allen
4935 Sunshine Lane
Sacremento, California 95841

International Windsurfer Sailing Schools
Michael Ross
1955 West 190th Street
Torrence, California 90509
Both of these groups conduct schools throughout the nation. Write for information and addresses of schools in your area.

Specialist Windsurfing Bibliography

American Practical Navigator, available through the Superintendent of Documents, U.S. Government Printing Office, Washington D.C. 02402.
Includes information on weather, navigation, as well as many charts.

The Rules Book, Eric Twiname (Scribner's) $5.95
Paul Elvstrom Explains the Yacht Racing Rules, Ed. by Richard Creagh-Osborne (De Graff) $6.50
Two small books that explain IYRU yacht racing rules clearly and concisely. Very useful to anyone who wants to go windsurfer racing.

Tactics and Strategy in Yacht Racing, Joachim Schult (Dodd, Mead & Co., Inc). A great introduction to racing tactics

Sailboarding: A Beginner's Guide to Boardboat Sailing, A. H. Drummond, Jr. (Doubleday) $4.95

Sailboarding, Peter Brockhaus and Ulrich Stanciu (Mayflower) $8.95

Windsurfing Results

Open Class Division 2 World Championship
1979 Guadeloupe.
Lightweight: Karl Messmer/Switzerland/Mistral.
Ladies: Marie Anick Maus/France/Tornado.

1980, Israel.
Lightweight: Karl Messmer/Switzerland/Mistral.
Heavyweight: Thomas Staltmaier/W. Germany/Mistral.
Ladies: Manuelle Graveline/France/Dufour.

1981, St. Petersburg, USA.
Lightweight: Stephan van der Berg/Netherlands/Tornado.
Heavyweight: Jan Wangaard/Norway/Sailboard.
Ladies: Maren Berner/Norway/Sailboard.

Windsurfer World Championship

1975, France
Light: Matt Schweitzer/USA.
Medium Light: Brian Tulley/USA.
Medium Heavy: Derk Thijs/Netherlands.
Heavy: Helgo Zarges/W. Germany.
Ladies: Susie Swatek/USA.

1976, Bahamas
Light: Robbie Naish/USA.
Medium Light: M. Garaudée/France.
Medium Heavy: Derk Thijs/Netherlands.
Heavy: K H Stickl/W. Germany.
Ladies: Susie Swatek/USA.

1977, Sardinia
Light: Robbie Naish/USA.
Medium Light: Nino Stickl/W. Germany.
Medium Heavy: Guy Ducrot/France.
Heavy: Anders Foyen/Norway.
Ladies: Claudine Forest-Fourcade/France.

1978, Mexico
Light: Robbie Naish/USA.
Medium Light: Matt Schweitzer/USA.
Medium Heavy: Anders Foyen/Norway.
Heavy: Johnny Myrin/Sweden.
Ladies: Bev Thijs/Netherlands.

1979, Greece
Light: Marc Nieuwborg/France.
Medium Light: Thierry Eude/France.
Medium Heavy: J. Salen/Sweden.
Heavy: Cort Larned/USA.
Ladies: Manuelle Graveline/France.

1980, Bahamas
Light: Karl Messmer/Switzerland.
Medium Light: Frederic Gautier/France.
Medium Heavy: Thomas Staltmaier/W. Germany.
Heavy: G. Long/USA.
Ladies: Manuela Maschia/Italy.

1981, Japan
Light: Mike Waltze/USA.
Medium Light: Robert Nagy/France.
Medium Heavy: Frederick Gautier/France.
Heavy: Johnny Myrin/Sweden.
Ladies: Manuela Maschia/Italy.

Pan Am Cup

1980
Robbie Naish/USA/Mistral Naish.

1981
Ken Winner/USA/Dufour.

1982
Robbie Naish/USA/Mistral Naish.

World Speed Record

1977
17.1 knots: Derk Thijs/Netherlands/light-weight Windglider.

1979
19.2 knots: Clive Colenso/UK/Olympic Gold.

1980
24.45 knots: Jaap van der Rest/Netherlands/TC Special.

1982
27.82 knots: Pascal Maka/France/Sailboard Maui-Ellesse.

The Open Class

Divisions 1 and 2
Divisions 1 and 2 (flatboard and round-board) have virtually the same measurement specifications, with the major exception of the depth of board: Division 1 is not more than 16.5 cm ; Division 2 is not more than 22 cm.
The full Division 1 and 2 rules can be obtained from the IYRU. They can be summarised as follows:
Overall length: 3920 cm max.
Beam at widest point: 630 mm min.
Other beam restrictions: Not less than 590 mm for lengths of 1300 mm.
Depth of board: not more than 165 mm.
Division 1: Not more than 220 cm.
Division 2: Weight of board: 18 kg min.
Daggerboard: 700 cm max depth from underside of board.
Skeg: 300 mm max.
Mast: 4700 mm max.
Buoyancy: The Division 2 board shall either have three watertight compartments dividing its total volume into approximately equal parts, or a minimum of 0.1 cubic metres of rigid closed cell foam. The Division 1 board shall be entirely filled with rigid closed cell plastic foam of approved density.
Safety: A towing eye and mast leash must be fitted. There shall be no sharp upward projecting edges of radius less than 15 mm.
Materials: High modulus fibres such as Kevlar are prohibited.
Footstraps: Prohibited.
Limitation of equipment: During a race meeting only one board, two sails, and two daggerboard may be used. The board shall not be altered in any way during the race meeting.
Harness: Permitted.
Compass: Prohibited.
Weight Groups: Two are recommended, up to and over 70 or 75 kg.

Division 1 and 2 Sails
Division 1 and 2 sails have the same specifications and are interchangeable:

Luff	4400 mm
Leech	4300
Head to mid foot	4300
¾ height width	940
½ height width	1680
¼ height width	2270
Foot	2580

Division 1 Homologation
Division 2 is open to any one-off prototype, or production board that satisfies the measurement rules.
Division 1 is restricted to:
A. An IYRU International Class ie. Windsurfer, Windglider, Mistral.
B. A class approved by the IYRU of which there are not less than 2000 similar boards satisfying the measurement rules. NB. When Division 1 was introduced into the UK in 1982, no classes (apart from the three International Classes) satisfied B. Therefore the RYA held 'flatboard trials' and homologated the following boards: Alpha Waikiki, Beacher, Comet, Dufour Wind, Hunter, Hi Fly 555, Icarus, Jet Surf, Klepper S3, Magnum 370, Mirage Aloha, Mistral Kailua, Mistral Naish, Reix 390, Rocker Regatta, Sailboard Carib, Sailboard Delta, Sailboard Grand Prix, Sailboard Sport, Sailboard Vario, Sea Panther, Yess.

Division 3
Open Class Division 3 covers tandems. The measurement specifications and class rules are similar to Division 2, with the very obvious exception that Division 3 allows two rigs and two drivers! There are also the following main differences:
Overall length: 6800 mm max.
Beam at widest point: Not less than 650 mm/ not more than 750 mm.
Depth of board: Not more than 250 mm.
Weight of board: 50 kg min.
Daggerboard: 910 cm max depth from underside of board.

Windsurfing Racing
International Yacht Racing Union Rules
The IYRU rules are complex and lengthy enough to need a book to themselves. Either of the two books suggested in the Windsurfing Bibliography are strongly recommended if you intend racing.

The rules for boards are the same as those used for yachts and dinghies with a few exceptions. This is not always ideal, as a windsurfer is very different from other sail craft, and in some cases regatta organisers such as WSP have drafted their own very much more simple rules to be used during their own events.

Index

Acknowledgements

Jeremy Evans would like to thank the following who have all helped in one way or another with this book: Will Sutherland of Windsurfing Professional; Peter Williams of Hayling Windsurfing and Chelsea Wharf Windsurfing; Dee Caldwell of Dee Caldwell's Sailboard Centre; Mike Lingwood of Surf Sales Ltd.; James and Jane Ellis of Poole Windsurfing Centre; and Pan Am for laying on windsurfing in Hawaii.

Thanks to Philip Clark and Julian Holland who made the book possible; and finally thanks to Lesley who was the most help of all.

Holland & Clark Limited would like to thank the following for their help in the preparation of this book: Brian Bailey and Miranda Smith for checking the proofs; Christine Dakers Kapteijn for translating the chapter by Jaap van der Rest; Diana Rosenberg of Mistral for translating the chapter by Karl Messmer; and finally the staff of Evans Brothers Limited for their patience and encouragement.

Photo Credits
Where not otherwise credited, photographs are by Alastair Black. Photographs from other sources appear on the following pages:
Chelsea Wharf Windsurfing: 38–39
Jeremy Evans: 43, 84, 86–87, 91, 107, 104
Hayling Windsurfing: 37
Mistral: 15, 16, 20 (below), 22, 76, 107 (below)
Sodim: 150, 151, 152, 153, 154, 155
Tabur: 157
Cliff Webb: 24, 25, 31, 35, 44, 73, 126, 128 (below),
    129, 130, 131, 132, 133, 137, 139, 140, 142, 145,
    147, 148